RETREAT RESOURCES

DESIGNS AND STRATEGIES FOR SPIRITUAL GROWTH

Volume Three: Retreats for Youth

RETREAT RESOURCES

DESIGNS AND STRATEGIES FOR SPIRITUAL GROWTH

Volume Three: Retreats for Youth

General Editor:
Maury Smith, O.F.M., D.Min.

Assistant Editor:
E. Jackie Kenney

Paulist Press

New York, N.Y., Paramus, N.J., Toronto, Canada

247.3
Sm62
V.3

204065

Copyright ©1976 by the Missionary Society of St. Paul the Apostle
in the State of New York

All rights reserved. No part of this book may be reproduced or transmitted in any
form or by any means, electronic or mechanical, including photocopying, re-
cording or by any information storage retrieval system, without permission in
writing from the Publisher.

Published by Paulist Press
Editorial Office: 1865 Broadway
                   New York, New York 10023
Business Office: 400 Sette Drive
                   Paramus, New Jersey 07652

Printed and bound in the United States of America

Library of Congress Catalog Card Number: 74-83719

ISBN: 0-8091-1910-2

Designed by Joanne Cossa and Anne Gayler

ACKNOWLEDGMENTS

Lyman Coleman, *RAP*. Waco, Texas, Word Books. Used with permission.

Robert Raines, *RESHAPING THE CHRISTIAN LIFE*. New York, Harper & Row, 1964. Used with permission.

"Happy the Man." Reprinted by permission of Franciscan Communications Center, Los Angeles, California. Sebastian Temple, Copyright © 1967.

"Prayer of St. Francis." Reprinted by permission of Franciscan Communications Center, Los Angeles, California. Sebastian Temple, Copyright © 1967.

"Arms Dealer for the World?" Reprinted with permission from *AMERICA*. February 19, 1972. All Rights Reserved. © 1972, America Press, Inc., 106 West 56th Street, New York, N.Y. 10019.

"Penance and the Law" by James F. Campbell in the February, 1972, issue of *THE PRIEST*, Our Sunday Visitor, Inc., Huntington, Indiana 46750. Used with permission.

Brian P. Hall, Religious Values Scale from "The Psychology of Change" in *ST. ANTHONY MESSENGER*, March, 1970. © St. Anthony Messenger, 1615 Republic St., Cincinnati, Ohio 45210. Used with permission.

DEDICATION   In Memory Of

REV. GERMAIN R. SCHWAB 1916-1969
Provincial of Midwest Franciscans

REV. FRANCIS LEO MADSEN 1920-1968
Vicar Provincial of Midwest Franciscans

Both of these priests were committed to the preaching apostolate.

SPECIAL THANKS   The editor wishes to thank all who participated in making this resource material an actuality. Special thanks go to Jackie Kenney who did the indexing and organization of the kit; to those in the Franciscan Community who encouraged and supported me: Charles Bloss, Paul Schullian, and Donald Betz. There were several typists, but I wish to thank Pauline Dossman, who did most of the typing, and our secretary, Jean Wawrzyniak, who was always there in an emergency. Finally, I would like to thank my friends, the Banets, Alperns, and Kleins, who have not seen much of me the last six months but who have been patient and supportive of this work.

CONTENTS (Volume 3)

CONTENTS (Volume 1)

CONTENTS (Volume 2)

INTRODUCTION

Welcome to Volume Three of Retreat Resources! Contained here are a selected group of retreat designs for use with youth groups.

Please refer to Volume One for a general introduction to the Retreat Resources series. Also, you will find there a section entitled "Part One: General Introductory Materials." This offers some basic ideas on how to give a retreat. The following specific areas are treated: Content Choosing Procedures, How To Design A Retreat, Scheduling, Administration, Evaluation Procedures, Bibliography on Preaching and Follow-Up Procedures.

Also, you will find at the end of this volume a complete cross indexing of all materials contained in three volumes of this series.

PART ONE: RETREAT DESIGNS

I. TEEN—MODERN: A VALUE CLARIFICATION APPROACH

by Rev. Charles P. Tobin

A. THEME/PARTICIPANTS

INTRODUCTION

BEHOLD THE TURTLE—HE ONLY MAKES PROGRESS WHEN HE STICKS HIS NECK OUT.

The theme of this unique model revolves around the concept of a turtle who can only move when he takes the risk to extend his neck, thus making himself vulnerable. If any value in our society has been neglected and ridiculed, it is that of vulnerability, even amidst much superficial discussion of openness. The turtle retreat dares a participant not to just talk about openness and wave a flag of self-disclosure, but to engage in some micro-experiences of risk-taking as called for by the Lord Jesus.

Most participants would probably envision a retreat to simply involve lecture input (often boring and at best, little remembered) and are rarely expected to become active participants in the retreat process. The medium of the turtle retreat ought to impress the participant as much, if not more than, its message. To be willing to engage in exercises and activities that expose and develop our values and our image of self demands a certain amount of candor and willingness on the part of the participant. But the results are more than rewarding, if the participant commits himself to a wholehearted venture into himself and the people around him.

To describe the theme of this model, therefore, is a difficult task in that the theme does not simply evolve from a summary of individual topics or materials, but incorporates the *process* that demands a certain amount of risk-taking, openness (in the sense of being willing to accept another's values and beliefs as they are), and vulnerability, which is the virtue of exposing oneself to living in the radical sense of Jesus' example.

To be vulnerable to life, that is to stick one's neck out, involves a time to be, a time to do (to do many things), a time to listen, a time to create, and a time to dare. The theme of this model calls for:

1. SEARCHING, QUESTIONING, COMPARING
   To ask why, to doubt, to be confused is a controversial scandal in today's Church that causes many parents and others to become agitated with modern approaches to religious education. However, the process of searching is as essential to the individual Christian as it has been to the entire Judaeo-Christian pilgrimage.

2. LEARNING, LISTENING, COMPARING
   Solid input, revealing the experiences and values of other cultures, is an important part of the turtle retreat.

Progress in the spiritual life comes easier when we profit from the similar decisions, goals and values of individuals, or of a people.

3. PRAYING, COMMUNICATING, DIGESTING
No matter what pat formulas may be presented to the individual, there will be no real progress until feelings and fears, doubts and decisions are tested on caring companions or on a patient and loving Father, either alone or in common.

4. AFFIRMING, SHOUTING, ENGAGING
A time comes when the neck must actually be extended and new-found convictions tried out. Experiences within the retreat ought to provide for such an affirmation whether via a talent experience, a love letter or another vehicle.

5. REJOICING, BEING, CELEBRATING
Vulnerability that brings progress demands proclamation. Mutual being leads to celebration, and that is— GOOD NEWS!

DESCRIPTION OF AUDIENCE THIS MODEL IS TO REACH

This value clarification model was used with sophomore, junior, and senior high school students and was designed for this audience. It could, however, be adaptable for college groups, discussion clubs, married couples, or any group that would be interested in a search for understanding themselves and others. Emphasis is placed on individual growth, group building, and spiritual mission. Read through the sessions and exercises carefully and decide if any changes should be made for a particular group.

It is not necessary for the audience to have had experience with group dynamics prior to the retreat. The retreat will provide the learning situation. (It is extremely helpful for group leaders to be informed or have some experience here.) However, expect groups familiar with the process to become a cohesive unit more readily and to approach the exercises with greater maturity than those who are not.

The audience should not expect a crash course in sensitivity methods and group dynamics. They should not expect to be spiritually overburdened. Nor should they look forward to a weekend of rap sessions designed to solve all of their personal inadequacies and the world's problems. For the retreat was not designed for any of these purposes exclusively. Rather, it offers a mutually inclusive balance of each.

B. OUTLINE/SCHEDULE

1. TURTLE RETREAT—OUTLINE OF CONTENTS

FRIDAY EVENING

Session I—Registration, Orientation, Welcome
    Exercise 1—Introduction of Oranges
    Exercise 2—Priorities List
    Talk—The Valuing Process
    Exercise 3—Group Games
           (a) Famous Person
           (b) Red Face
    Exercise 4—Symbolic Scavenger Hunt

Session II—Track I—Senior, Junior
    Exercise 1—Evaluating Objectives
    Exercise 2—Pantomime
    Interview

Session II—Track II—Sophomore
    Exercise 1—Film—"To See Or Not To See"
    Exercise 2—Value Continuum
    Exercise 3—Film—"Up Is Down"
    Interview

SATURDAY MORNING

Session III—Beatitudes
    Exercise 1—Evaluating My Attitudes
    Exercise 2—Making Right My Attitudes

Session IV—Relationships
    Exercise 1—Evaluating My Relationships
    Exercise 2—Making Right My Relationships
    Exercise 3—Trust Walk

SATURDAY NOON

Session V—Penance
    Exercise 1—Film—"Right Here, Right Now"
    Talk—Person of Jesus
    Exercise 2—Penance Service

Session VI—Creating and Relating
    Crafts, Decorating, Planning Sessions, Rap Sessions

SATURDAY EVENING

Session VII—Sharing
    Exercise 1—Small Group Sharing and Evaluation
    Exercise 2—Individual and Group Talent
    Liturgy

SUNDAY MORNING	*Session VIII*—Film—"Baggage"
	Exercise 1—Evaluating My Life-style
	Exercise 2—Making Right My Life-style

SUNDAY AFTERNOON	*Session IX*—Love
	Exercise 1—Letters
	Exercise 2—Response
	Exercise 3—Evaluation

Session X—Closing
    Exercise 1—Film—"A Time To Die"
    Scripture Reading

2. CONTENT THEMES

Information on the Turtle Retreat

BIOGRAPHY

INTRODUCTION

DESCRIPTION OF AUDIENCE THIS MODEL IS TO REACH

GENERAL DIRECTION ON HOW TO USE THIS MODEL

TURTLE RETREAT—OUTLINE OF CONTENTS

OUTLINE—CHRONOLOGICAL APPROACH

RETREAT SCHEDULE

COMMENTS ON ADMINISTRATION PROCEDURE

SAMPLE OF THE PRE-REGISTRATION FORMS

SAMPLE OF THE CONFIDENTIAL LETTER TO PARENTS

MATERIALS NEEDED FOR THE RETREAT

RESOURCE BOOK LIST

RETREAT INTERVIEW

EVALUATING MY OBJECTIVES

EVALUATING MY ATTITUDES

MAKING RIGHT MY ATTITUDES

EVALUATING MY RELATIONSHIPS

MAKING RIGHT MY RELATIONSHIPS

EVALUATING MY LIFE-STYLE

MAKING RIGHT MY LIFE-STYLE

INDEX CARDS ON ALL GAMES

INDEX CARDS ON ALL FILMS

INDEX CARDS ON ALL EXERCISES

INDEX CARDS ON ALL TALKS

EVALUATION

IDEAS FOR FOLLOWING UP THE PROGRAM

3. *RETREAT SCHEDULE*

FRIDAY   *SESSION I*

6:30 p.m. Registration, Orientation, Welcome
Singing

Exercise 1
7:00   Introduction of Oranges

Exercise 2
7:30   Priorities List
List twenty things you like to do
Move into theme values
8:30   Introduction of Staff
Break into groups

Exercise 3
8:45   Group Games
(a) Famous Person
Along with this have student give his name,
year in school, parish, and repeat name of
person who spoke before him.
(b) Red Face

Exercise 4
9:15   Symbolic Scavenger Hunt
Break into semi-groups. Satisfaction, Warmth,
Frustration, Insecurity.
Retreat Council
Group selects one student representative for
council.
Theme Song
10:00   Break

SESSION II—Track I (Auditorium)

Exercise 1
10:15   Evaluating My Objectives
Reaction Time

Exercise 2
Pantomime
11:00   Prayer Session
11:15   Interview
During interview, students will stay in auditorium.

SESSION II—Track II (Cafeteria)

| | *Exercise 1* |
| 10:15 | Film—"To See or Not To See" |

Exercise 2
Value Continuum

Exercise 3
Film—"Up Is Down"

| 11:00 | Prayer Session |
| 11:15 | Interviews |

  During interview, students will remain in cafeteria.

12-12:20 a.m. Staff Meeting—only group leaders need to attend.
 12:00 a.m. until ....

  OPTIONS: Gym (closes at 3:30 a.m.)
      Cafeteria
      Dorm
      Auditorium

SATURDAY 8-8:30 a.m. Breakfast
       Retreat Council Prayer Meeting (Chapel)
    8:50 Singing

SESSION III

9:10 Beatitudes

Exercise 1
Evaluating My Attitudes (small groups)

Exercise 2
Making Right My Attitudes (small groups)
10:15 Break

SESSION IV

10:20 Relationships

Exercise 1
Evaluating My Relationships (small groups)

Exercise 2
Making Right My Relationships (small groups)
Singing
  When groups have finished previous activities, music director will lead singing.
Group leaders only will meet in staff room.

Exercise 3
Trust Walk
12-12:30 p.m. Lunch

1:15-1:30	Prayer Session

SESSION V

1:30	*Exercise 1* Film—"Right Here, Right Now" Talk—Person of Jesus
2:00	*Exercise 2* Penance Service—Rags
2:30	Break

SESSION VI

2:50-3:00	Crafts Explanation of Evening
3:00-4:00	FIRST Expression NOTE: Each group leader must create some expression. Alternates may do so if they wish.
4:00-5:00	SECOND Expression
5:00	Sport Activity Decorations for Cafeteria Liturgy Planning
6:15	Dinner
7:15-8:00	Free Time Rap Sessions, Confessions, Liturgy Planning, Clean-Up, Finish Craft Projects.
8:00	Singing

SESSION VII

8:15	*Exercise 1* Small Group Sharing and Evaluation. Small group will choose winner for prize.
9:00	*Exercise 2* Total Group Talent
11:00	Mass
12:00 a.m.	OPTIONS: Auditorium—Film Cafeteria—Music Gym—Closes at 2:30 a.m.

SUNDAY	8:00 a.m.	Breakfast Retreat staff will eat together.
	8:30	Singing

SESSION VIII

9:00	Film—"Baggage"

10:15	*Exercise 1*
	Evaluating My Life-style
	Exercise 2
	Making Right My Life-style
11:30	Lunch
12:00 p.m.	Singing

SESSION IX

12:15	Talk—Love
	Exercise 1
	Letters
	Exercise 2
	Response
	Exercise 3
	Evaluation
2:00	Singing

SESSION X—Closing

	Exercise 1
	Film—"A Time To Die"
	Scripture Reading
	Theme Song
2:30-3:30	Group Clean-Up

C. GUIDELINES

1. GENERAL DIRECTIONS ON HOW TO USE THIS MODEL

Specific directions are given at the beginning of each session or exercise. Depending upon the size and age level of the group, the following suggestions may be suited to one's needs. See administrative procedure for other comments.

DIRECTOR

Select, elect, or appoint a director for the retreat. This person is responsible for the organization and implementation of the retreat. During the retreat the director will set the pace, give directions, select options, or make any changes necessary.

COORDINATOR

The director may wish to select a coordinator whose responsibility would be to act as a clearing house for the various operations and activities taking place before and during the retreat. The coordinator is responsible for having equipment, materials, and supplies available, checking schedules, and assisting the director in the retreat process.

STAFF

Try to have at least one *adult* staff person for every ten participants. If possible, get two. This would provide a group leader and an auxiliary leader in each group of ten participants. If at all possible, insist that the group leaders be available the entire weekend. This is very important for the group.

GROUP LEADERS (ADULTS)

Select group leaders carefully. Of paramount importance should be their sincerity and desire to be an effective member of the group. If the group leaders are not familiar with the group dynamic or valuing process, one may want to have some preliminary staff meetings to explain, explore, and experience these concepts. One may even want to go through some of the retreat exercises. It is the task of the group leader to work himself out of a leadership role and to function as just another member of the group. For this reason, it is not necessary for him to be familiar with the exercises, films, talks, etc. One may wish to direct the group leaders to some of the books listed in the bibliography. *At least* make sure that they are aware of some cardinal rules for group discussion:
(a) Don't interrupt.
(b) Don't ridicule or criticize.
(c) Don't give advice.
(d) Don't judge.
(e) Be sensitive to special needs of individuals.

PARTICIPANTS

All participants should stay the *entire* weekend. Make very few exceptions to this rule.

GROUPS

It is wise to divide participants into groups according to age level as well as one can. Try to get a suitable proportion of boy/girl, familiar/unfamiliar, lively/non-lively in each group. Assign one group leader, plus one auxiliary leader, to each group of seven to ten participants.

TALKS

The theme of each talk is given on the index card. The director need not (and probably should not) give all the talks. If so, assign a person his talk well in advance of the retreat. The talk outline is only a guide. Choose options, ideas, or themes suitable to one's needs.

PRAYER SESSIONS

Prayer sessions are indicated in several places on the schedule. These are optional and may be with the entire group, small groups, or with several people. One may choose conventional prayers, Scripture, or spontaneous prayers. It could be held in the chapel, around a table, or outside under a tree. It is recommended that one at least make the effort to try some prayer sessions. Don't forget the power of the staff praying as a group in preliminary meetings.

RETREAT COUNCIL

The director and/or staff should meet with an elected retreat council several times during the retreat. Get some feedback. Ask questions that will determine how the retreat is going (e.g., How do participants in the group feel? How is it going in the group? Is help needed in any way?). Ask the retreat council to help with any problems that may exist in their group. Perhaps members of the council will have to assume a leadership role. Inform them of upcoming events; let them know of any need and welcome their help.

STAFF MEETINGS

Staff meetings should be held at various intervals also and for the same purpose. Find out how other groups are progressing. Are the groups moving too fast—too slow? Should any changes be made? These meetings should be short and can be held with the director and/or coordinator.

INFORMATION

Have a *folder* available for each group leader which contains the retreat schedule, group lists, description of films, games, and other materials used during retreat. Also, for each participant have a folder with his name on it which includes only a roster, blank paper, and song book (optional). Do not include a schedule. As the retreat progresses, he will be given the exercise work sheets, which can be kept in his folder.

(NOTE: Each packet can be assembled with a participant's name on it from the pre-registration and group lists. One might want to color code them per each group. As the retreat breaks up into groups, the coordinator can distribute packets to the group leader, who in turn gives them to the group members.)

AUDITORIUM

Decorate the meeting area with banners and posters reflecting the theme of the retreat. (NOTE: Make a special banner: "Behold the turtle—he only makes progress when he sticks his neck out." See sample sketch included.)

CAUTION: Check to be sure the room is large enough so that one group will not disturb another. If possible, check with a box company that may be able to supply large pieces of corrugated board. Ideal size is 75" x 75", scored in the middle. Use about eight sheets of corrugated. Punch four holes down the sides and join together with yarn. These can be used very effectively as dividers; they insure privacy, and each group will enjoy decorating its "home."

GIFTS If possible, try to arrange for each participant to receive some small retreat remembrance. In this retreat, participants were given a small wood-carved turtle attached to a thin leather strap. These were placed around their necks during the peace rite of the Mass. Another suggestion is *Good News for Modern Man*, the New Testament, published by the American Bible Society, at a very small cost. Have the group leader write a note to each member of his group and present each with the book. Participants will want other group members to sign their book also. It is an effective remembrance.

PRIZES If one includes the talent show in the retreat, prizes might be offered. A few suggestions: books such as *Reach Out, The Gospel According to Peanuts, The Little Prince, Interrobang, New Jerusalem Bible*, etc., turtle candles, turtle key rings, turtle patches, turtle jewelry, turtle stationery, etc.

MUSIC Make music a part of the retreat. It's very effective for getting everyone together, setting the tone for upcoming sessions, and building community spirit. Try to find someone who plays the guitar to be music director. You may want to have song books available. Also, during some of the exercises one might want to have suitable recorded music in the background.

2. COMMENTS ON ADMINISTRATION PROCEDURE

The retreat will be much more effective for staff and participants if most of the work is done before the actual retreat begins. Plan ahead and try to anticipate any special problems that might occur. The following suggestions, along with the general directions, may be adaptable to one's own retreat.

LODGING Estimate the number of participants and staff who will attend the retreat. Where will the retreat be held? It is psychologically important to be away from the normal environment. Can the number be accommodated? What about transportation? (Most young people have sleeping bags and are content to sleep on the floor.) What about kitchen facilities, craft rooms, auditorium, and chapel?

PRE-REGISTRATION   Via mail or some method, distribute a letter inviting prospective participants. Attach a registration slip that can be returned. With young people, it is wise to have a parent sign this slip, thereby giving permission for the person to attend. (See pre-registration sample.) Set a registration deadline of at least 2½-3 weeks.

COST   The cost of the retreat will vary depending on lodging, meals, and financing. See items to consider:
   (a) How much does it cost per person, per day at retreat site?
   (b) Are meals furnished? How much per meal? Plan and prepare meals oneself?
   (c) Will the parish or organization finance part of the cost?
   (d) How much can the participant afford to pay?

MEALS   If one must prepare one's own meals, it will involve a special headache. The following suggestions are recommended after trial and error:
   (a) Do not take this project on yourself. Find *someone* whose *sole* responsibility is menu planning, purchasing, and cooking.
   (b) If necessary, assist the person in getting auxiliary help. This is not too difficult; a surprising number of parents are willing to spend a few hours helping prepare a meal.
   (c) Don't expect *staff* to help with meals. They need this time to relax, to visit, and interact with participants.
   (d) However, each group could be assigned a meal at which it would assist in the serving or cleaning-up process. Using paper plates, cups, etc., makes clean-up a simple task.

LETTERS   If one uses the letter idea in Session IX, a lot of cooperation will be needed—BUT TRY IT!
Theme: Love—communication—generation gap.
Materials needed: A letter from the parents addressed to their son/daughter, explaining why they love him/her.
Directions:
   (a) Send a *confidential* letter to the parents explaining the retreat and asking them to write a personal letter to their child telling why they love him/her. Instruct them that they are *not to tell their child.* (See sample letter enclosed.)
   (b) Have a large manila envelope for each group. List the group names on the front. As letters come into the office for participants, mark the name off the front and place in envelope. They will be ready for distribution when needed.
   (c) Double-check lists/letters to be sure *everyone* has a letter. It might be necessary to call a few parents to get the letters.

FILMS A special note on films. All films were obtained through the local library at no cost. The St. Francis (TeleKetics) films were obtained through the area Religious Education Office of the Diocese at a nominal fee. If possible obtain films in the same manner. If this is not feasible, see index card which lists distribution company and rental fee.

D. TALKS/EXERCISES

2. SESSION I

Session I—Registration, Orientation, Welcome.

THEME

To welcome those attending the retreat.
To finalize registration.
To officially open the retreat.

SETTING

Large auditorium. Casual, informal atmosphere where people can sit on the floor.

MATERIALS

Pre-registration list/group list.
Registration table with name tags already made up. (see option A.)
Proper audio equipment, depending on size of room.

DIRECTIONS

Utilize warm familiar music as a means of welcome. Request staff to welcome and assist participants. As participants arrive have them take any personal belongings to the dorm areas. As they enter the main auditorium, the registration table should be directly inside the door with name tags available. Indicate each participant's presence on group list.

The director should call the meeting to order and welcome the group. The coordinator can then finalize registration lists if necessary. (Leftover name tags may indicate an absence.) Watch for people who did not pre-register; they will have to be assigned to a group. Any other announcements, ground rules, etc., should be given at this time. Time for the first exercise. (See option B.)

Option A—Participants might make their own name tags and perhaps decorate them. If so, paper, marking pens, scissors, etc., will be needed. Have participants check in at registration table and then proceed to an area set aside for name tags.

Option B—Take everyone's watches. Have several staff members in the middle of the room with gummed labels. Put name on the label and attach it to the back of the watch. Put watches in box and keep them in a safe place. Return to participants just before closing ceremony. This is a time for thinking, reflecting, searching. It's a time to forget about time.

Session I—Exercise 1

Introduction of Oranges.

| THEME | To serve as an icebreaker. |
| | To sharpen awareness. |

THEME To serve as an icebreaker.
To sharpen awareness.

MATERIALS Oranges or tangerines.

DIRECTIONS Have oranges laid out on table at the back of the room. Instruct each person to take one. Then:

(1) In *silence*, they are to introduce themselves to their orange and become familiar with it.

(2) Find another person (encourage participants to find someone they don't know) and introduce their orange to someone else's. (Option: allow them the opportunity to trade their orange with this person.)

(3) Place *all* oranges in the center of the room.

Reaction Pause. Ask for volunteers:

(a) How do you feel at this point?

(b) How do you feel toward your orange?

(c) Did you hate to give it up? Why?
(Option: Did you trade it? Why?)

(d) Do you see any relationship between your feelings and the orange? (E.g.: Do you feel that you're just like everybody else here? Just another orange? Is your orange different? How? Are you different? In what way? Do you feel lost? Would your own friend recognize you in a crowd?)

(4) Everyone is to find *his* orange.

(5) Decide if you want to keep your orange; do you want to eat it yourself or share it with a friend?

(6) Reaction Pause. Ask for volunteers:

(a) Were you afraid you weren't going to find your orange?

(b) Are you *sure* you have your orange?

(c) What did you do with it?

(d) Tell us about your feelings and your orange.

PROCESS This game provides a warm-up exercise for the group. It gives them a chance to meet new people, to increase their awareness of everyday things that surround them, and forces them to think about themselves in relation to everyone else.

After the exercise, one may wish to gather up the remaining oranges. Very few will eat their orange and some will want to take theirs home.

Session I—Exercise 2

Priorities List.

THEME Serves as an introduction to, and an explanation of the value approach theme used throughout the retreat.

MATERIALS   Paper and pencils for everyone.

DIRECTIONS   In complete *silence*, list twenty things you like to do. Allow the group three to five minutes to complete this. Then use the following:

(a) Put a 21 beside any item you think you will still be doing at age 21.
(b) Put an A or P beside each item, indicating whether you would like to do it alone or with people.
(c) Put a C or U beside each item, indicating whether it is conventional or unconventional to your peer group.
(d) Put a J beside any item connected with your job or role.
(e) Put a K beside any item you would want your children to be doing.
(f) Put a D or a W beside each item, indicating whether you do it daily or weekly.
(g) Put a P beside any item you take pride in doing.
(h) Put a C, F, or E, indicating that you like to do the item because of church, family, or educational training.
(i) Put a 65 if you'll be doing any item after retirement.
(j) Put a 5 if you weren't doing the item five years ago.

PROCESS   Allow the participants a few minutes to examine their lists. This is a good examination of their life-styles. Some will be surprised at the shallowness of their lives. Others will be amazed that they won't enjoy doing certain things five years from now; or that they will not want their young doing these things. Question (h) will point out quite clearly that most of the things they enjoy doing *do not* come from church, family, or education.

The previous exercise leads into the first talk and theme—The Valuing Process.

Session I—Talk

NOTE: The person giving this address should be referred to *Values and Teaching*, by Raths, Harmin, Simon, Charles Merrill Publishing Company, Columbus, Ohio. See Chapter 3, Values & Valuing.

THE VALUING PROCESS

THEME   Persons have experiences; they grow and learn. Out of experiences may come certain general guides to behavior. These guides tend to give direction to life and may be called values. *Our values show what we tend to do with our limited time and energy.* Different experiences give rise to different values. Values evolve and mature as experiences evolve and mature.

A. The Process of Valuing—Seven Criteria
   All seven must apply before we call it a value.

Based on three processes: choosing, prizing, acting.
  (1) Choosing
      (a) freely
      (b) from alternatives
      (c) pondering consequences of each alternative
  (2) Prizing
      (a) cherishing, being happy with the choice
      (b) willing to affirm the choice publicly
  (3) Acting
      (a) doing something with the choice
      (b) repeatedly, in some pattern of life
B. Value Indicators
   Some things indicate the presence of a value but are different from a value. We call these expressions which approach values, but do not meet all the criteria:
   (1) Goals or purposes
   (2) Aspirations
   (3) Attitudes
   (4) Interests
   (5) Feelings
   (6) Beliefs and convictions
   (7) Activities
   (8) Worries, problems, obstacles

Introduction of Staff—Break into Groups

THEME

To acquaint the staff with the group.
To divide into small groups.

MATERIALS

Group lists, folders, corrugated board.

DIRECTIONS

1. Depending upon its size, one may have the director introduce the staff, or each person could introduce himself individually.
2. From the group list, the director or coordinator should announce the name of each group leader and members of that group. Each group should then assemble in a small circle. (If you have folders available for the participants, they should be distributed now.)
3. Try to have a large enough room so that each group will have the opportunity to interact without disturbing other groups. (NOTE: See suggestion in General Directions. If corrugated is used, now is the time to "build your home.")

Session I—Exercise 3

Group Games: Famous Person—Red Face.

THEME

Self-disclosing. To give each group the chance to become acquainted.

MATERIALS	None.
DIRECTIONS	*Famous Person*

1. The group leader proposes that *each person* tell about a famous individual that he knows or has read about or desires to be like. He should be encouraged to elaborate quite a bit on the character, morals and values of this individual. When everyone has finished, move on to Red Face.
2. Each member of the group tells about an embarrassing situation that happened to him or something he regrets having done.

PROCESS
These are two very important exercises. Take sufficient time for them. This is the first encounter a person has with other members of the group. The games are intended to be self-revealing, enabling the participant to learn something about a person's inspirations, values, and feelings. Some suggested questions: How do you feel? How did you feel about that? What would you do if the same situation reoccurred? How do you compare with this person?

Session I—Exercise 4

Symbolic Scavenger Hunt.
(from *Breaking Free*, by Lyman Coleman; Word Inc., Pub.)

THEME
To help one identify the things that give rise to four basic emotions in life—and to share these discoveries with others.

MATERIALS
None.

DIRECTIONS

1. Participants should hunt through the contents of their purse or billfold for various tokens to symbolize the following emotions in their lives: (a) satisfaction, (b) frustration, (c) warmth, (d) insecurity.
2. Break into semi-groups or groups of two or three. Participants should get with someone they don't know very well. One person can explain all four of his symbols to the others, or each can share the symbol he selected for satisfaction, then for frustration, etc. Explain in detail why a particular symbol was selected. Give background.
3. Participants should reassemble with their groups. Each person should introduce another member of the smaller group by explaining one interesting or unusual symbol that he selected. Explain something about the person that was discovered through his choice of symbols. (Option: Select one emotion. Have each person explain his choice of symbol to the group.)
4. At the close, each group should try to form a circle of love and celebrate its experience together in some way—song, word, prayer.

PROCESS   This exercise is intended to help the group members become better acquainted with each other, to set the pace for honesty and openness, and to build a spirit of community.

Retreat Council—Before the groups break up, each group should select one person to be its representative on the retreat council. See general directions.

This concludes Session I.

3. SESSION II

Session II—Depending upon the size and age of the group, one might want to split the groups for the next two exercises. Some younger members may not be ready for one or would find the other too threatening and react accordingly. We offer a separate track for them which takes place at the same time *but in another room.*

Session II—Track I (e.g., for Seniors, Juniors).

Exercise 1—Evaluating Objectives (from *Rap*, by Lyman Coleman; Word Inc., Pub.).

THEME   To enable you to evaluate your hopes and aspirations in the light of Scripture and share results with a small group.

MATERIALS   Pencils and copies of Evaluating My Objectives for everyone.

DIRECTIONS   You will reflect upon your life in view of the teachings of Jesus in the Sermon on the Mount.

1. The Scripture passage describes the role of the Christian in the world as being like salt and light. It is possible that you have never stopped to consider the implications of your life-style. Here is the challenge of this session. Read the passage slowly, pausing along the way to let the Holy Spirit speak to you.
2. When you are through, fill out the Reflection Questionnaire. Phase One deals with the Scripture passage. Phase Two deals with you. The questionnaire is not a test of skill. There is no right or wrong and no grade at the close. It is simply a tool to focus your thoughts.

PROCESS   Do not force this session. People need time to focus their thoughts on Scripture, on Christian community, on their objectives. The reaction time is very important.

Exercise 2—Pantomime (from *Breaking Free*, by Lyman Coleman, Word Inc., Pub.).

THEME   The object of this exercise is for everyone to get in touch with his own inner feelings and then to communicate these feelings nonverbally to the group.

MATERIALS   None.

DIRECTIONS
1. Sit close together in groups of four.
2. If there is room on the floor for everyone to lie down and completely relax, this would be ideal. Otherwise, simply slump back in your chair.
3. Close your eyes and allow your mind to explore the world of your inner feelings. Simply ask yourself: "How do I feel at this moment in my life?" One dominant feeling may come to mind, such as confusion or insecurity. Or possibly a variety of emotions will come to mind, such as great joy and freedom on the one hand and fear and anxiety on the other.
4. After a few minutes, the leader will call time and a person in each group is to pantomime what he is feeling. For instance, if you are feeling up-tight and insecure, you might wring your hands and put your hands to your head. If you are overflowing with joy, you might smile and throw up your hands in ecstasy. If your feelings involve other people, for instance, if you are distrustful, you may glance hurriedly at those in your group and then put the palm of your hand toward them.
   (NOTE: The leader may demonstrate his feelings and ask the group to guess what he was trying to convey.)
5. In each small group of four, the viewers are to explain what the pantomime communicated to them. Then the person who presented the pantomime explains what he meant. One of your group may have recognized your feelings perfectly, or they all may have missed them.
6. Follow the same procedure for each person.
7. In the groups that finish early, ask each member this question: "If you could change one thing in your life, what would you change?" The answer could be anything from a flaw in one's personality to a situation in the home—but it should be personal.
8. At the close, form a circle of love and celebrate your experience together in word, prayer or song. However, because this session has been an experience in nonverbal expression, you may want to have your celebration wordless as well. You may want to celebrate by a clasp of the hand, a look in the eye and a slap on the shoulder—but it should be real.

PROCESS   Some will find this exercise a little awkward or embarrassing. Some participants may need help with this. Question seven is very personal, but at this point the group should have established a sense of trust, belonging, and community.

Session II—Track II (e.g., Sophomores).

Exercise 1—Film—"To See or Not To See."

THEME　　Merits of illusions.

MATERIALS　　Movie projector, extension cords if necessary.

DIRECTIONS　　1. Show film. Let group react.
　　　See index card for possible discussion questions.

PROCESS　　See index card for evaluation. Film is intended as an introduction for next exercise.

Exercise 2—Value Continuum (from Value and Teaching, by Sidney Simon, Charles Merrill Publishing Co., Columbus, Ohio).

THEME　　To show that most issues have many possible alternatives.

MATERIALS　　Newspapers or magazines—radical and reactionary.

DIRECTIONS　　1. Select a controversial issue to be discussed with the groups (e.g., censorship, abortion, amnesty, etc.).
　　2. Place the two extreme positions at opposite ends of a line on a chalkboard. This is a value continuum.
　　3. Each group is to go through newspapers or magazines, identify other positions in the same issue and try to place them on the continuum, both in relation to the poles and to positions already placed.

PROCESS　　One of the main criteria for values is a consideration of alternatives. The importance of the value continuum is to demonstrate that issues are not always black or white. Point out the need to look at alternatives and their consequences.

Session II—Track II

Exercise 3—Film—"Up Is Down."

THEME　　Tolerance, conformity.

MATERIALS　　Projector, screen, extension cords if necessary.

DIRECTIONS　　Show film. Let groups react. See index card for possible questions.

PROCESS　　This short film is a good follow-up and closing for this exercise. See index card for further ideas.

PRAYER SESSION　　The different tracks could come back together for a short prayer service before concluding the evening's activities and beginning the interview; or each track can have a separate service and proceed with the interview. See general directions for further notes.

Interview

THEME

To give the group leader and each member of his group an opportunity to meet privately, to become better acquainted, to learn more about themselves.

SETTING

Quiet place with table, two chairs.

MATERIALS

Interview Sheet.

DIRECTIONS

1. The group leader is to interview each person in his group. (NOTE: If you have an auxiliary group leader, you may divide the interviews.) *See option.*
2. The group leader directs the questions to the person being interviewed and writes his responses on the interview sheet. (NOTE: Do not let the participant see or fill out the questionnaire—tends to become too impersonal and mechanical.)
3. The group leader keeps the interview sheet. He may wish to look them over when all the interviews are completed. When he is finished with them, they should be given to the director or coordinator.

PROCESS

The interview presents the best opportunity for the group leader and participant to have an in-depth conversation and get better acquainted. Do not rush the interview. It was purposely placed late so that time would not be a factor. Try to find a quiet place. Be *sure* everyone in each group is interviewed. Do not expect the person to have all the answers available. Give him time to think. Do not pressure him or criticize his responses. Look over the interview sheet when it is finished. Pay particular attention to question 7. Is there a problem in the group? Does one particular person need help? How can the leader help him?

OPTION: Director or coordinator may wish to interview the staff for some of the same reasons as mentioned above.

This concludes Session II.

4. SESSION III

SESSION III—Beatitudes—Talk.

THEME

Beyond the law, the threshold of commitment.

The beatitudes of Christ are perhaps the most misunderstood and yet the most important of Christ's words to us. Before we understand the concept of the beatitudes as new law, we ought to understand the "old law"—the threshold of what the Father expects us to be and to do.

The beatitudes (the Sermon on the Mount) seems to have been described by the Gospel writers in direct comparison to the old law (the Ten Commandments). With the old law, the Father presents ten prescriptions to the people's leader, Moses, and the law is given on the sacred mountain to indicate their centrality and importance as the foundation of the old covenant between God and his people. The old law consists of specific directions for living life which are very clearly enunciated as basic premises for living a good life. The new law, as presented in the beatitudes, is probably vague both as to the number of beatitudes given (Gospel writers do not agree.) and as to the role of law in the new covenant—Jesus provides descriptions of what would make one happy rather than a codex of no-nos for the people. It is clear that at least one of the Gospel writers wished to present the beatitudes as a parallel to the Ten Commandments, so much so that he probably falsified the account of him speaking to the people on a plain and indicates that Jesus was on a mountain, or at least a hill, in order that the comparison with the giving of the Ten Commandments on a mountain might be more evident.

So why a new law, if indeed that is what the beatitudes are—law? Mankind matured and evolved just as clearly as any person grows up and becomes more mature and more adult. Under the old covenant, the Father treated his people in a childlike fashion with specific directions and clear-cut rewards and punishments. Jesus, however, calls his friends and the people he loves to an adult relationship with the Father and presents a new kind of "law."

A parent, in raising a young child, has to tell the child a hundred times a day to do this, or not to do that, to wipe his feet when he comes in the door, not to throw his coat on the floor, not to scream because the baby is sleeping, not to eat cookies before supper, to share his toys with others; the list could go on—and does. But hopefully a day comes during late adolescence when a parent can simply say to little Johnny: "Be a gentleman"—and from that point on Johnny will begin to do things that are thoughtful and courteous, without his parents needing to remind him, or even being around to suggest a particular course of action.

So too, with God the Father—he no longer has to tell us a hundred times a day (if we are mature in our religion) to do this, or not to do that, as he would in the Ten Commandments. The regulations and "laws" for the modern Christian are simply considered as minimums, as the bare threshold to religious life. But it is the call by Jesus, to the style of happiness described in the beatitudes, that challenges us to become adults (to be gentlemen) in our relationship to the Father who loves us so deeply. Thus, with this kind of description of happiness as proclaimed in the beatitudes, it is not necessary that we number them because we ought to be adding and developing our own list of comparable events in our lives that produces this happiness. You have been called then to do so much more than the minimum law of the old covenant, but the new law of Jesus' covenant with us is so special, indeed unique to our circumstances, gifts, opportunities, and friendships that it could never be codified except as it is done by you, as you listen to the Holy Spirit, as you hear the word of Jesus, and as you long for the Father in a lifelong search for the best way to serve him as the person you are.

Session III—Exercise 1

Evaluating My Attitudes.
(From *Rap*, by Lyman Coleman, Word Inc., Pub.)

THEME   To enable participants to evaluate attitudes about their present circumstances in the light of Scripture.

MATERIALS   Pencil, work sheets—Evaluating My Attitudes.

DIRECTIONS   You will reflect over your life in view of the teachings of Jesus in the Sermon on the Mount.

1. The Scripture passage on back of the work sheet (also known as the beatitudes) deals with the radical life-style of the followers of Jesus as far as their attitude or outlook on life is concerned. Read it slowly, pausing along the way to think about the meaning of each phrase for your situation.
2. When you are through, fill out the Reflection Questionnaire. Phase One deals with the Scripture passage. Phase Two deals with you. The questionnaire is not a test of skill. There is no right or wrong and no grade at the close. It is simply a tool to focus your thoughts.
3. Move into groups of four persons each, preferably with others whom you do not know very well.
4. To get started, everyone, in turn, shares what he circled for the first point in Phase One of the questionnaire and explains why. The *why* will force you to deal with the reason behind the response—which is more important than the response itself.
5. Then everyone shares his thinking on the second point, etc., until each has gone through all of Phase One.
6. The object of Phase Two of the session is to celebrate life together. In a word, to "be" a real Christian community—caring, sharing, bearing up each other in love, trust, and acceptance.
7. Pause a few minutes to allow those who did not finish Phase Two of the questionnaire to do so.
8. Depending upon the time schedule, you can decide to stay in groups of four or move into groups of eight.
9. Each person, in turn, explains how he would complete the first point in Phase Two. Then everyone explains the second point, etc., until the exercise is completed. Here is the heart of the

session. Up to this point, everything has been theory. Now, it is for real.
10. At the close, join together in a circle of love and celebrate your experience together in song, word or prayer.

PROCESS   For many people "beatitudes" is just a word, the meaning of which may be a bit cloudy in their minds. This exercise is a spiritual encounter with the beatitudes—made very personal.

Session III—Exercise 2

Making Right My Attitudes.
(From *Rap*, by Lyman Coleman, Word Inc., Pub.)

THEME   To deal with the basis for Christian life-style from the viewpoint of Scripture.

MATERIALS   Pencil, copy of Making Right My Attitudes.

DIRECTIONS
1. In silence, read over the Scripture passage for the session, pausing after each verse to jot in the margin one of the following symbols:
   * if you understand the verse clearly
   ? if you have a question about the meaning
   † if you get special inspiration from the verse
   ‡ if you really get convicted about something in your life
   You can draw more than one symbol for each verse, but you must have at least one for each verse.
2. Ask yourself the question: "Which two verses speak to my need or my situation?" Underline them.
3. Then, in the top-left corner of the work sheet, write the number of the first verse you have chosen and draw a circle around it. Read the verse again, and starting with the first part, rewrite it in your own words.
4. When you have finished with the first underlined verse, write the number of the second verse you underlined and put a circle around it. Then proceed to rewrite this verse in your own words in the same way—expanding on the deeper meaning of the verse for your life and situation.
5. When ten minutes are up, regardless of whether everyone is through with his paraphrase, move on to the application.
6. Ask yourself the question: "As far as these two verses are concerned, what is the thing I must work on in my life?" It can be anything from a bad attitude at work to a broken relationship with your wife, but it should be honest and specific—very specific.
7. Whatever comes to mind as the need in your life at the moment, jot it under the word *application* at the bottom of your work sheet. It does not have to be long; just a few words will do, such as "screaming at the children."

8. Then, under the *need* put down three things you can do about it during the next week. If screaming at the children is the problem in your life, you might jot down: Tell them I am sorry when I scream at them. Ask their help. Commit the problem to God.

9. Gather together in groups of four and have one person in each group serve as the moderator. His task is to see that the discussion stays on the subject and the material is covered. The role of moderator should rotate to a different person at each session.

10. The moderator asks each person in the group to explain which verses he picked for his paraphrase—and why. (The why will be interesting in itself.) Then those who have paraphrased the first verse in the passage read aloud what they have written. As each paraphrase is read, the moderator should listen for something that would be good for "gut level" discussion. He can then come back with a question that focuses the discussion on this area. For instance: "Bill, what did you mean by 'uptight'?" or "Helen, would you mind giving me an example out of your own experience to clarify what you mean?"

11. After four or five minutes move on to the next verse that has been paraphrased and do the same.

12. Follow this procedure verse by verse through the passage until all of the verses that have been paraphrased have been covered—or until the thirty minutes are up.

13. In the small groups each person in turn shares his application, explaining the thing he wants—needs—to work on in his life and what he is going to do about it.

14. After the sharing, gather together and form a circle of love. In oneness and dependence, pray specifically for each other, using the first person—I, me, my.

PROCESS   This is a Bible-study exercise as well as an opportunity to reinforce the spiritual encounter prior to the exercise. Notice that group process is also a part of the exercise.

This concludes *Session III.*

5. SESSION IV

Session IV—Relationships—Talk.

THEME   Constancy of relationships.

MATERIALS   *The Giving Tree*, by Shel Silverstein, Harper & Row Publishers.

DIRECTIONS   Read the story slowly and clearly and, if possible, use the illustrations in the book as it is read (perhaps on an overhead projector).

TALK

The tree gives, and gives, and gives until it is only a sad little stump and yet offers even that to the boy. But aside from the constancy on the part of the tree, perhaps the important thing to reflect about and to ponder would be that the giving by the tree does not consist in external gifts, such as beautifully wrapped birthday presents, but involves the unique gift of self which is perhaps the rarest gift and best gift that we can give to another person in any relationship.

You have all known people who give of their material gifts or who love to wrap beautiful packages, or who delight in demonstrating their power in doing favors for others because of their positions. But the tree simply gives of itself in directed ways to the actual needs of the other, namely the boy. But the constancy of giving, as well as the uniqueness of giving of self, are also joined by a third reflection that the giving is never directed toward any return or any expectation from the other.

In our humanness, we might question whether these three ideals of giving, in any relationship in which we are involved, are really possible. Does it ever happen in life that people give to the extent and in the style that the tree does, but then too, do we ever have to be perfect in attaining that ideal before we begin to imitate the beauty of the tree, or the depth of Jesus, or the example of friends we know who even begin to approach these three ideals of:

1. constant giving?
2. total giving of self?
3. giving without return?

Session IV—Exercise 1

Evaluating My Relationships.
(From *Rap*, by Lyman Coleman, Word Inc., Pub.)

THEME

To enable you to evaluate your present relationships in the light of Scripture.

MATERIALS

Pencil, copy of Evaluating My Relationships.

DIRECTIONS

You will reflect over your life in view of the teachings of Jesus in the Sermon on the Mount.

1. The Scripture passage on the work sheet sets forth for the followers of Jesus a whole new basis for dealing with interpersonal relationships, conflicts and hostilities. Read the passage slowly, pausing along the way to think about the meaning of the words for your life.
2. When you are through, fill out the Reflection Questionnaire. Phase One deals with the Scripture passage. Phase Two deals with you. The questionnaire is not a test of skill. There is no right or wrong and no grade at the close. It is simply a tool to focus your thoughts.

3. Move into groups of four persons each, preferably with others whom you do not know very well.
4. To get started, everyone, in turn, shares what he circled for the first point in Phase One of the questionnaire and explains why. The *why* will force you to deal with the reason behind the response—which is more important than the response itself.
5. Then everyone shares his thinking on the second point, etc., until each has gone through all of Phase One.
6. The object of this part of the session is to celebrate life to-gether. In a word, to "be" a real Christian community—caring, sharing, bearing up each other in love, trust and acceptance.
7. Pause a few minutes to allow those who did not finish Phase Two of the questionnaire to do so.
8. Depending upon the time schedule, you can decide to stay in groups of four or move into groups of eight. If you have only twenty minutes left, stay in groups of four. If you have thirty minutes, move into groups of eight.
9. Each person, in turn, explains how he would complete the first point in Phase Two. Then everyone explains the second point, etc., until the exercise is completed. Here is the heart of the session. Up to this point, everything has been theory. Now it is for real.
10. At the close, join together in a circle of love and celebrate your experience together in song, word or prayer.

PROCESS   This is another spiritual encounter providing reflection questions that help people relate Scripture to their own experience.

Session IV—Exercise 2

Making Right My Relationships.
(From *Rap*, by Lyman Coleman, Word Inc., Pub.)

THEME   To deal with the basis for Christian life-style from the viewpoint of Scripture.

MATERIALS   Pencil, copy of Making Right My Relationships.

DIRECTIONS   NOTE: The directions for this exercise are identical with those for *Session III, Exercise 2*—Making Right My Attitudes.

PROCESS   See *Session III, Exercise 2.*

Session IV—Exercise 3

Trust Walk.

THEME   To increase sensory awareness, to rediscover exploring, to build a spirit of trust among the group.

MATERIALS	Blindfolds.
DIRECTIONS	The group pairs off. One of each pair is blindfolded and the other walks him around the building and/or grounds by guiding from behind. *No words are spoken.* The leader has the blindfolded partner experience touching, smelling, feeling various objects.
PROCESS	The results of this exercise are varied. But the procedure is simple, the content light, and most will enjoy the exercise before the noon meal.
OPTION	In conjunction with the trust walk, have a trust meal. Similar to the trust walk, one partner guides the other to the dining hall, assists him through the cafeteria line, but doesn't indicate to him what foods they are selecting. The meal is then commenced with the one blind partner being assisted by the other, with reflections upon the texture of food, the helplessness of lack of sight, and the care exerted by the seeing partner.

This concludes *Session IV.*

6. *SESSION V*

Session V—Christ/Penance—Exercise 1

Film—"Right Here, Right Now."

THEME	Search for God.
MATERIALS	Projector, extension cords if necessary.
DIRECTIONS	Show film. Let groups react. See index card for details, possible questions, evaluation. Film is used as an introduction to the following talk.
TALK	
THEME	The incarnation of Jesus, the radical presence of the man through others.

Jesus was present to the people in the Gospels in many and varied ways. In his humanness, he continually surprised individuals who expected him to think, act, and perform in certain conformed patterns. Jesus' whole message was that he would not exist in a physical temple, or even in conformed styles of behavior.

The Holy Spirit, through the Vatican Council and current theology, has continually challenged our routine images of the *presence* of Jesus in today's Church and world. There was a time when we could be certain that Jesus lived in the tabernacle and that he wouldn't bother us at home, or call us at the office, or bug us at inconvenient times. "Right Here, Right Now" and other forms of media are reminding us that Jesus lives; he lives not just in the tabernacle but in his people and speaks through his word and relates through the signs of bread and wine in the Eucharist when he becomes one with us.

So the question is: Where does Jesus exist for you? Through whom does he speak? How does he relate and live for you now? Do you see him alive and present in people who have needs? How skilled are you in hearing, as well as seeing, the needs of those around you? Part of the effort of this retreat has been to enable you to begin to recognize the radical presence of Jesus in the people around you, to question your relationship to those with whom you associate in family and other surroundings. The elusive question that you attempt to face becomes: "Have I missed the presence of Jesus in the simple and ordinary relationships within my life that become so routine and sometimes so agonizing and difficult that I seek instead the presence of Jesus in the grand and glorious tabernacle of the temple where, at least, I feel I can know he is present as he ought to be?" Jesus scandalized the Jewish people of his age simply by being himself and by not being the magnificent king and Savior who always worked in extraordinary and divine ways. So look around you—where do you see him at work? Bend your ear to the ground; where do you hear him speaking? Reach out; what kind of hand will he use to reach back to respond to you?

Our relationship to Jesus is two-fold. Let us not forget that we are a part of his body; that indeed we are his body. Therefore, we need to incarnate (to make present) him to others for that is indeed what he has called us to do, to be the sign of him at work among us. He continuously reminded us that if we are nice only to those who are nice to us, that we have failed him and simply equated us with those who do not believe. Thus, in the reaction time following this talk, take a while to react to the following two concerns:

1. How, and in what way, is he present in my life?
2. How have I made him more present, more real, in the relationships in my life?

Session V—Exercise 2

Penance Service.

THEME   Forgiveness.

MATERIALS   Small branch of tree (mount on wood frame or place in a bucket of sand), small strips of cloth for each person (use an old sheet).

TALK   The story is told of a young college student who has left his Kansas home and gone to the West Coast to experience life and to get away from the "home scene." Having decided that the West Coast was empty of real life, and realizing that he would like to return to his home, the boy boards a train and heads back toward his small-town Kansas home. A middle-age businessman boards the train in Colorado and sits next to the boy, realizing that he is intently looking out the window for a particular landmark. Questioning the lad, the businessman inquires as to where the boy is going and why he is so intently peering out the window. The young man relates that having spent the money given to him by his father, he is on his way home and has wired his father that he is returning. The businessman, still puzzled at the young man staring out the window, asks him more directly what he is looking for. The young man says: "I am not certain how my father feels about my returning, since he was so upset that I left home. I told him, in the wire, that if he wanted me to get off the train at home, that he should tie a white rag to a branch of the old apple tree close to our house, that you can see as we enter the town." As the train moved quickly toward the small village, and familiar landmarks began to be seen, the boy buried his head and began to cry. The concerned man, asking if he could help in some way, was told by the boy to watch for him and tell him if the white rag was anywhere to be seen in the crippled, old apple tree, just outside town. As the train sped into the station, the man put his arm around the boy in a paternal and gentle way and said: "Son, not only was there one rag in the tree, but the old apple tree had a bright, rippling rag flying from every single branch, to welcome you home."

The story of the rags, like the prodigal son story in Scripture, indicates the deep forgiveness and loving relationship of our Father in Heaven. Forgiveness, like both sides of a rag, involves our realization that we have been forgiven by the Father and by others, and on the other hand that we need to forgive others who have hurt us. No action in life is more difficult than that of forgiving another who has hurt us and yet surely no action in life is more rewarding, or promising of peace, than when we have been forgiven by another. The beautiful and central prayer of the Christian (the Lord's Prayer) correctly ties the Father's forgiveness to our willingness to really and completely forgive one another.

In the following exercise, as you take some time to reflect upon one person whom you need to forgive and one person who, perhaps, ought to forgive you, utilize your time to examine your close relationships and realize that no one is really "at home" until he is at peace with another.

DIRECTIONS

1. Tell the story "Rags."
2. Each person is to take his strip of cloth. On one side of the cloth he is to write the name of a *person whom he needs to forgive* for some reason. On the other side of the cloth he should write the name of a *person who needs to forgive him* for a reason.
3. Each person takes his cloth and puts it on the tree.

PROCESS

"Rags" is a touching story which appeals particularly to teenagers. They can identify with the story. Writing a name on the

34

cloth creates a powerful lesson for penance/forgiveness and the *need to express* that feeling. NOTE: Keep the tree; it should be used at the penitential rite during the liturgy.

Following this exercise, priests should be available for confessions.

This concludes *Session V.*

7. *SESSION VI*

Session VI—

Creative Expression.

THEME

To create, to reflect, to plan, to interact.

MATERIALS

All of the craft materials listed on supply sheet, plus any others one may wish to include.

DIRECTIONS

1. Instruct the participants that in the time remaining before dinner, they are to create two expressions of an idea, theme, or feeling *that has been generated by the retreat* (e.g., candles, woodblocks, poems, songs, mobiles, etc.).
2. Stress the fact that this is not "free time," "arts and crafts," etc. *The expression must relate to the retreat.*
3. The first expression should be done on an *individual basis.* However, the *second* expression should be done by several people or *as a group* (skit, slide presentation, song, etc.).
4. Explain to participants that these expressions must be shared with individual groups and voluntarily with the entire group at the evening session.
5. If prizes are to be used for the evening session, one may want to display some of them. Also, take this time to organize a judging committee. This could consist of three members of the retreat council, plus two adult leaders.
6. Explain that any remaining time could be used for liturgy planning, decorating for dinner, sport activity, confession, freshening up, etc.

PROCESS

The schedule for the remainder of the day is very light, but the group will be ready for a diversion. The time is not wasted, particularly if one *stresses that the craft must express an idea or feeling from the retreat.*

The remainder of the time is an important time for sharing and relating with others.

Various staff members or auxiliary people should be in charge of some of the areas of interest—liturgy planning, decorating, candle-making, mobiles, slides, etc. They may have to offer assistance on some projects. Be sure to have suitable working area for these projects.

A NOTE ON DINNER

If possible, try to make the evening meal a special one. Create a warm atmosphere, using candlelight, soft music, place-mats, tablecloths, place-cards, decorator plates, cups, etc. (These could be made by participants and decorated.) Try to avoid the cold sandwich, hot dog or hamburger menu. It will be more work, but get some parents to help. If a committee decorates the dining hall, keep it as a surprise for the others. The participants will love it. It's another way to say: "You're special!"

This concludes *Session VI*.

8. SESSION VII

Session VII—Sharing—Exercise 1

Small Group Sharing.

THEME | To let each person share his creation with his group.

MATERIALS | Items that have been made by individuals, prizes.

DIRECTIONS | 1. Each person in the group shares his creation and explains how he made it and why. What theme is represented in his craft?
2. Each small group selects the person whose craft best reflects some thought, theme, or feeling generated by the retreat.
3. When everyone is finished, each small group winner should share his craft before the entire assembly and be awarded a small prize.

PROCESS | This is an opportunity for each person to share some creation with others, however small or insignificant it may be. Be sure one stresses at the beginning of craft period that everyone will share his expression with others, and perhaps be awarded a prize. This will create additional interest and motivation for the craft period.

Session VII—Exercise 2

Group Talent.

THEME | To provide each group the opportunity to share with others.

MATERIALS | Items prepared by group, prizes.

DIRECTIONS | 1. The format here can vary considerably. Use whatever process you desire. One might have each group share its creation before the assembly. Judging committee could award prizes to winning group.

2. Ask for volunteers whether individual, couples, participants, staff, etc., to share an expression, thought, feeling, or emotion that has been generated by the retreat themes or exercises. One may want to award a prize for the best selection.

PROCESS   This session is enjoyable and relaxing. Some of the creations will be impressive; others will wish that they had done better. Watch for some spontaneous creation or expression—especially on the staff level. Expect some of the talent as not reflecting the themes of retreat. If prizes are awarded, the judging should reflect this.

This concludes *Session VII.*

9. THE LITURGY OF THE WORD

The liturgy committee should have the songs, music, themes, etc., planned. Invite the group around the altar. Pause at the prayers of the faithful and invite their petitions. Give them some time—they should be ready to share at this point. (At one retreat, at the sign of peace, the celebrant presented each participant a small wood-carved turtle on a leather strap. One may wish to give some small remembrance of this retreat.)

Homily

THEME   Giving—"The Son of Man came to serve, not to be served."

In *The Giving Tree*, we saw the theme of the tree giving its ultimate, all that it had, to the other. Complete and unrestrained giving seems to have been a part of Jesus. He continually repeated the essence of his servant theme (to serve, not to be served) in various ways to different groups. He gave of himself to people like Mary Magdalene and yet called her to a tremendous growth of giving. And even though he gave a man like Peter the great gift of keys, the very gift demanded a life of giving, even unto death (a gift of complete life) on Peter's part.

What gifts has he given you? When was the last time that you itemized or became more conscious of his giving? Do you see his gifts as completely free or, like the keys, do they by their very essence demand or call forth a giving on your part? When others give to you by means of the talents or gifts that he has given them, how do you respond? Is it good that gifts are given with no strings attached, or does the very act of giving—the medium of giving—always call forth a response, a giving, a renewed *yes* from you, no matter what the gift, no matter what the message of the giving medium?

Maybe then the servant theme of Jesus is simply calling you to a whole life-style of giving and maybe we need to look closer at what real giving implies in today's society. A life-style of giving obviously implies more than simply giving of gifts, which is fun, exciting, and rewarding to us as individuals. A life-style of giving may even mean that we need to learn how to receive—to receive well the gifts of sharing, of concern, of values that others would wish to give to us. Many a teenager needs not so much to give better, in the strict sense, to his parents, but to develop the art or skill of receiving from others. It is precisely this which will be the best form of giving.

Develop the skill of real giving and you will have gone far toward understanding the implementing-the-servant theme of Jesus. The turtle makes progress only when he sticks his neck out and we too will only begin to live when we begin to risk giving, despite consequences, despite past experiences, despite a recipient's worthiness, or despite our own lack of vision. Re-evaluate your giving patterns and you will find yourself actually re-evaluating your relationship to the Lord Jesus.

Alternative

THEME   Self-Giving (via the medium of dialogue homily).

Rather than use a canned homily, it would be more valuable to utilize the medium of a dialogue homily in order that the participants themselves might more beautifully share and reinforce their own convictions and feelings concerning the theme of giving. It should be suggested that the celebrant of the Eucharist allow the students to either reflect upon the Gospel reading, which might be the Suffering Servant ("I came to serve, not to be served.") or to provide a couple of leading questions concerning their own attitudes toward Jesus' giving. Most celebrants find a dialogue homily difficult in that they themselves are uncomfortable with silence and often end up making most of the comments themselves, or feel that they should elaborate on the student's comments. However, the goal of the dialogue homily is to draw forth the feelings and values of the students which ought to involve as much participation on their part as possible.

10. SESSION VIII

Session VIII—Life-style.

Film—"Baggage."

THEME   Man's struggle for freedom.

DIRECTIONS   Show the film. Let groups react. See index card for description, evaluation, possible questions. Film is an introduction to the following exercise.

Session VIII—Exercise 1

Evaluating My Life-style.
(From *Rap*, by Lyman Coleman, Word Inc., Pub.)

THEME   To enable you to evaluate your commitment to Jesus Christ in the light of Scripture.

MATERIALS   Pencil, copy of Evaluating My Life-style.

DIRECTIONS   You will reflect over your life in view of the teachings of Jesus in the Sermon on the Mount.

1. The Scripture passage on bottom of work sheet describes two hypothetical builders, one who built his life-style on a rock and another who built his life-style on the sand. Jesus used this parable at the close of the Sermon on the Mount to summarize his teaching. Read the passage slowly, pausing along the way to let the Holy Spirit speak to you about your life-style.
2. When you are through, fill out the Reflection Questionnaire. Phase One deals with the Scripture passage. Phase Two deals with you. The questionnaire is not a test of skill. There is no right or wrong and no grade at the close. It is simply a tool to focus your thoughts.
3. Move into groups of four persons each, preferably with others whom you do not know very well.
4. To get started, everyone, in turn, shares what he circled for the first point in Phase One of the questionnaire and explains why. The *why* will force you to deal with the reason behind the response—which is more important than the response itself.
5. Then everyone shares his thinking on the second point, etc., until each has gone through all of Phase One.
6. The object of this part of the session is to celebrate life together. In a word, to "be" a real Christian community—caring, sharing, bearing up each other in love, trust and acceptance.
7. Pause a few minutes to allow those who did not finish Phase Two of the questionnaire to do so.
8. Depending upon the time schedule, you can decide to stay in groups of eight. If you have only twenty minutes left, stay in groups of four. If you have thirty minutes or more, move into groups of eight.
9. Each person, in turn, explains how he would complete the first point in Phase Two. Then everyone explains the second point, etc., until the exercise is completed. Here is the heart of the session. Up to this point, everything has been theory. Now, it is for real.
10. At the close, join together in a circle of love and celebrate together in song, word or prayer.

PROCESS   As the group approaches the end of the retreat, it is fitting that they examine their life-style in this spiritual exercise and in *Exercise 2.*

11. *HOMILY II*

THEME   Uniqueness of the person.

MATERIALS	One long-stem red rose, to be held in the hand of the speaker.
TALK	In the beautiful and familiar story of the Little Prince, you will remember that the Little Prince comes to the planet earth from another planet, where he had been the friend of a beautiful flower that had always told him that she was unique in all the world. The Little Prince visits a garden and, upon walking into the garden, discovers hundreds of roses, identical to the flower he left on his planet. Disappointed and upset, he hears the fox tell him that his rose is still unique, special, in all the world. For it is the time that he had wasted, in caring for his rose, that had made her unique and so dear to him.

In an age of computers and the reduction of a person to one long serial number, it is necessary to hear again the comforting words spoken to the Little Prince. Maybe you have forgotten that you are unique. Maybe it has been some time since someone has told you that you are different, in a good and healthy way. Maybe others have not been careful enough to act toward you, and respond to you, in a way that clearly indicates that you are special, that you are precious, that you are cherished, that you have worthwhile and specific contributions to make, that you are an individual, that you are worth nourishing, that you are loved. In an age when time becomes so precious to us, it hits you very hard when another person indicates that he has no time for you, but in the contrary vein, it ought to hit you just as hard when people, who otherwise have great difficulty telling you they love you, take, or make the time, to provide for you, to prepare for you, to help you, to give to you, to cry with you, to rejoice with you, to listen to you, to correct you and to call you to growth, to take pride in you, or to simply *be* for you. You are unique in all the world and the beautiful rose is an apt symbol of all of the time and care that is often lavished on you, in order that you may be transformed into the beautiful, unique and important person that you are. Take some time today to thank someone who has wasted time on you.

Session VIII—Exercise 2

Making Right My Life-style.
(From *Rap*, by Lyman Coleman, Word Inc., Pub.)

THEME	To deal with the basis for Christian life-style from the viewpoint of Scripture.
MATERIALS	Pencil, copy of Making Right My Life-style.
DIRECTIONS	NOTE—The directions for this exercise are identical with those for *Session III, Exercise 2.* Proceed in the same manner.
PROCESS	See Process—*Session III, Exercise 2.*

12. SESSION IX

Session IX—Love.

TALK

THEME

Importance of expressing love.

MATERIALS

Record, "Sometimes," by the Carpenters; record player.

DIRECTIONS

Because love is such a personal topic, it is extremely important for the talk to be very personal, which means that there is no way that one can pick up an index card and simply read a talk about love effectively or meaningfully. Yet since the format calls for an outline on the talk, one is presented below; but hopefully it will be adapted by the person giving the talk.

Play the record, "Sometimes." Allow a few moments of reflection before beginning to speak.

Sometimes—not often enough—we pause to try to say "thank you" to those who have loved us in some way. Both the words "thank you" and "I love you" are probably used all too infrequently in life by most people. It takes so little time, no matter how difficult it may be, to say "thank you" or to respond to love that is given freely to us, yet Americans especially, in an emotionally dulled society, find that it is almost impossible to adequately express the love that they feel. American men especially find our society saying to them that it is unmasculine to show their feelings, to cry, to reveal weakness, or to communicate love with gentleness and with constancy. Many a father has a very difficult time in simply bursting forth with the beautiful words: "Hey, I really love you"—to a son or a daughter, and sometimes finds the same difficulty in daily communicating the same, by words or by gentleness, to his spouse. When was the last time that someone joyfully and easily said to you: "I love you"—and how was it said? Was it in words—the simplest way and perhaps the most important —or was it in a gentle action, or a caring thought, or possibly in a routine duty or a very ordinary and expected way? Parents probably have trouble in verbalizing their love to you and assume that all that is necessary is that they carry out the responsibilities they have toward you in the routines of daily life. Yet every person has a need to hear the words: "I love you"—with constancy and with depth of meaning.

But if it is true that every person needs to *hear* the words: "I love you"—it is also true that every person needs to *say:* "I love you"—to another. It is indeed interesting that the extent of our love of God often depends upon our experiences of having been loved and our ability to respond with love to others in a mature and stable relationship. If we are in love with a caring God (a real Father), we will find that even though God may not need to hear us, we may need to cry out to him with all our power, the beautiful words: "I love you"—and we need to hear those three words echo back from the Father through the loving relationships that we have with others. Maybe we need to learn the art, the skill, of saying: "I love you"—more often to those around us and to the Father.

Rod McKuen's by-line states something like: "It matters not who you love, or how you love, only that you love." On the contrary, I think it does matter who you love and how you love, and that that love is always rooted in the love of the Father. But having said that, maybe the whole thrust of the turtle retreat is simply that you do love. Let us now take some time to really think about the people in our lives and about when we will next say: "Hey, I really do love you!"

Session IX—Exercise 1

Letters.

THEME   Love, communication, generation gap.

MATERIALS   A letter from parents for each participant. See administrative procedure for details.

DIRECTIONS   In silence, each participant should be given a letter from his/her parents.
Allow sufficient time for reading and reflecting on the letter.

PROCESS   This is a very effective exercise. Too often young people find it difficult to understand their parents. Few parents can recall the last time they said: "I love you," to their teenage child. Expect some tears at this point. Do not rush the session. If possible try to have it in the chapel with the participants sitting around the altar. CAUTION: *Be sure you have a letter for each participant.*
OPTION—Director may write a note of thanks to each group leader and distribute it at this time. Or have the group leader's spouse, children, friend, etc., write a similar *Confidential* letter of love to them. Distribute at this point.

Session IX—Exercise 2

Response.

THEME   To allow participants to reply to their parents' letters.

MATERIALS   Paper, pencils, envelopes.

DIRECTIONS   1. In silence, participants are to write a *confidential* letter to their parents explaining why they love them.
2. When finished, participant will place the letter in an envelope and address it to the parents.

3. *Letters should be collected* by the director or coordinator, who is responsible for mailing them.

PROCESS   This is a follow-up to the previous exercise and is included for some of the same reasons. One may want to do this exercise in the dining hall where participants can write at tables. Post and mail the letters as soon as possible. The retreat staff may never know it, but there will be many parents who will cherish their letter for a long time.

Session IX—Exercise 3

Evaluation.

THEME   To allow participants to react to the retreat.

MATERIALS   Pencil, paper.

DIRECTIONS   After participants have finished writing their letter, have them write a reaction to the retreat. Get their reactions to: the retreat in general, films, talks, exercise, food, staff, cost, etc.
What was the high point of the retreat?
What did they learn most from the retreat?
Would they come again?

PROCESS   This exercise is an opportunity for participants to have their say. Keep these evaluations; read them after the retreat is over. They could be very helpful in planning future retreats.

13. SESSION X

Session X—Closing.

THEME   To officially close the retreat—to consider the end.

Exercise 1—Film—"A Time To Die." (See index card for details.)

THEME   Death, resurrection, life, security.

MATERIALS   Projector, extension cords if necessary.

DIRECTIONS   1. Show the film. No discussion should follow—merely let the audience experience it.
2. Read the passage from Scripture—Ecclesiastes 3. ("For everything there is a season, and a time for every matter under heaven. . . ." *or* Isaiah 43:1-3a, 4-5a, 18-19a.)

PROCESS   As one comes to the end of the retreat, it is only fitting to look at the ultimate end. The message is very impressive. All weekend everyone has been learning how to live; is it too late to learn to die?

E. MATERIALS/RESOURCES

MATERIALS NEEDED FOR RETREAT

paper
pencils (a couple for each participant)
Scotch tape
masking tape
yarn
staplers
scissors
paper clips
crayons
Magic Markers
construction paper
glue
straight pins
rubber bands
pipe cleaners
envelopes (enough for each person)
small branch of tree
strips of cloth (enough for each person)
oranges/tangerines
posters
banners
films—"A Time To Die," "Baggage," "Question," "Right Here,
        Right Now," "To See or Not To See," "Up Is Down."
tape recorders, tapes
overhead projector
movie projectors
prizes for talent evening

CRAFT ITEMS
wood blocks
tissue paper
starch
hair spray
rocks
bottles
wax
candle molds (milk cartons, cottage cheese containers, etc.)
wick, color, scent
paints
tempera powder
burlap
felt
telephone cable

wire hangers
Any Craft Items—Suggestions?

In addition to the above, you will need one copy of each of the following for each participant making the retreat:

Evaluating My Objectives
Evaluating My Attitudes
Making Right My Attitudes
Evaluating My Relationships
Making Right My Relationships
Evaluating My Life-style
Making Right My Life-style
Interview
Good News for Modern Man

A TIME TO . . .

SENIOR HIGH RETREAT—April 28, 29, & 30

Behold the TURTLE . . . he only makes PROGRESS when he sticks his neck out.

A TIME TO . . . LEARN

To learn more about your faith,
more about you,
more about your people,
the Church.

A TIME TO . . . SHARE

To share concerns, doubts, ideas,
thoughts and feelings.

A TIME TO . . . QUESTION

To ask, to seek, to wonder,
even to share doubts, whys and
look at our confusion.

A TIME TO . . . THINK

To think about life, about love,
about caring, about breaking out of self,
about many things, about Him.

A TIME TO . . . PRAY

To pray alone,
to pray together,
to ask about prayer,
to share concerns about prayer.

A TIME TO . . . CELEBRATE

To celebrate life,
to celebrate His love for us,
to celebrate gratitude in Eucharist
together.

A TIME TO . . . AFFIRM

To say yes, to share beliefs,
to encourage, to enthuse,
to lead, to follow, to go forth.

YES, A TIME TO *REGISTER*—We need all sophomores, juniors, and seniors to have registrations in by April 7, along with the $10 fee.

Please complete the following registration form and return it to Father Tobin at St. Mark's Center, 3736 Lee's Summit Road, Independence, by April 7.

RETREAT RESERVATION FORM—April 28, 29, 30

I wish to reserve one share in the Turtle Retreat to be held at St. John's Campus, beginning 6:30 P.M. Friday, April 28, and ending 2:00 P.M. Sunday, April 30.

I will bring my own sleeping bag (bedding) and casual clothing.

(Signed)_____

NAME_____ PHONE _____

ADDRESS _____ PARENTS _____

_____Senior _____Junior _____Sophomore

_____$10 fee enclosed (includes room and meals)

_____Payment arranged with Fr. Tobin or staff

Please answer on the back of the reservation form:

Why are you coming to the retreat? (25 words or less)

PARENTS' LETTER—SAMPLE

CONFIDENTIAL TO PARENTS

Date

Dear _____

Congratulations! It is with great pride that we welcome your student to this year's retreat; to reflect and ponder over Gospel attitudes, values and needs of today's Christian. We are happy for you.

A retreat can be a very important time in a person's life. Decisions are often made, values and attitudes changed, friendships made, and a better concept of Christ received. For many students, it is an opportunity to become closer to dedicated couples and individuals, religious, and priests.

Because it is such an important time for your student, we would like to ask your help. Would you *write a personal letter* to your student, explaining why you love him/her?

The letter may be brief or lengthy; from one parent or both. It should be placed in a sealed envelope with the student's name on the front and mailed in an envelope to us, at _____, or given to any member of the retreat staff. Because of the nature of the experience, please *do not tell your child* that you are writing the letter.

God's work depends upon the prayers and support of his people; we need you to pray for the success of this retreat that God may touch the life of your child.

Sincerely yours in Christ,

P.S.: Please have your letter returned by _____

NAME: _____   CALL ME: _____
PARISH: _____   GRADE _____ RETREAT GROUP #_____

TO BE READ: The following is confidential to the staff and is simply a way to get to welcome you, know you better, to offer any help; to say, "WE CARE!"

(Answer on the back where needed)

1. Your favorite color? _____ Your favorite song? _____

2. Are you honest? _____ When was the last time you weren't? _____

3. Name one person who has been a tremendous influence in your life. _____
   Why?

4. Complete the following:
   (a) When I have free time, I mostly just _____
   (b) The Mass in our parish _____
   (c) The thing that irritates me the most about myself is _____
   (d) The thing that makes me different from everyone else here is _____
   (e) My best quality is _____
   (f) To value something means_____
   (g) I value _____

5. The two most important people in my life right now are
   1. _____ Because _____
   2. _____ Because _____

6. In my family, the person I am closest to is _____
   and the person I find hard to understand is_____

7. About my retreat group:
   (a) In my group, I feel _____
   (b) The person most helpful in our group is_____
   (c) The person having the hardest time is _____
   (d) The purpose of our group is _____

THANK YOU!

EVALUATING MY OBJECTIVES

PHASE ONE   1. The thought of being "salt for all mankind" and "the light for all the world" is something that (circle one):
      (a) leaves me cold   (b) frightens me
      (c) grabs me   (d) blows my mind

2. According to this passage, the Christian community should be a force in history by its (rank 1 to 4 in order of importance):
   _____ individual purity
   _____ radical life-style of love

_____ involvement in the needs of society
_____ separation from society

3. In my estimation, the reason why the Christian community I am a part of is not a force in society is that we don't intimately know (circle one):
(a) God (b) each other (c) the Scriptures
(d) the needs of society

4. I find the quotation by Robert Raines—see below—(circle one):
(a) right on target (b) off base a little
(c) way out in left field

PHASE TWO

1. My present objectives in life are:

2. The person or experience that has had the greatest influence in shaping my present thinking is:

3. What brings me the greatest personal satisfaction is:

"A servant people inevitably becomes a witnessing community. When we identify ourselves with the sufferings of others who have no observable claim on us, the world takes note . . . The leaven which was hid cannot be concealed any longer; the light is seen to be shining in the darkness; there is a community as obvious as a city set on a hill"—Robert Raines.

MATTHEW 5:13-16

You are like salt for all mankind. But if salt loses its taste, there is no way to make it salty again. It has become worthless; so it is thrown away and people walk on it. You are like the light for the world. A city built on a hill cannot be hid. Nobody lights a lamp to put it under a bowl; instead he puts it on the lamp-stand, where it gives light for everyone in the house. In the same way your light must shine before people, so that they will see the good things you do and give praise to your Father in heaven.

EVALUATING MY ATTITUDES

PHASE ONE

1. My first impression when I read the Scripture passage was (circle one):
(a) ho-hum (b) ouch (c) wow
(d) right on (e) whoopee

2. The word "happy" in this passage might be defined by the words (circle one):
(a) good fortune brought about through chance circumstances; lucky
(b) inner peace in the midst of painful or annoying experiences

(c) joy that springs from an inner possession
(d) contentment that comes from prior knowledge
(e) gratification of inner desires; pleasure, bliss

3. Of the eight beatitudes, the areas where I am strongest (mark with a plus) and the areas where I am weakest (mark with a minus) are:
—————— spiritually poor (to admit that you have needs, to be open to change, to realize that you don't have it all).
—————— mourn (to feel for the hurt of others, to empathize with others because you know what it means—you have been there).
—————— meek (to enable others to be themselves, to open up, to be quiet enough to hear others).
—————— spiritual hunger (to have your priorities in spiritual perspective, to have spiritual goals and motivations).
—————— show mercy (to have compassion without conditions, sensitive and responsive, freely, unconditionally giving yourself).
—————— pure in heart (to be in touch with your inner self, unencumbered by false images, honest with yourself, God and others).
—————— peacemaker (to bridge differences without destroying others' uniquenesses, to harmonize, to bring togetherness).
—————— endurance (to be able to accept hostility and anger without fighting back, to act rather than react in circumstances).

PHASE TWO

1. From what I have observed of the others in my group, I would say that the beatitude in which each person is strongest is (jot the name of each person in your group underneath the trait he has manifested):
Spiritually poor _____
Mourn _____
Meek _____
Spiritual hunger _____
Show mercy _____
Pure in heart _____
Peacemaker _____
Endurance _____

2. I would like those in my group to help me in my life to (finish the sentence):

MATTHEW 5:3-10

Happy are those who know they are spiritually poor: the Kingdom of heaven belongs to them!
Happy are those who mourn: God will comfort them!
Happy are the meek: they will receive what God has promised!
Happy are those whose greatest desire is to do what God requires: God will satisfy them fully!
Happy are those who show mercy to others: God will show mercy to them!

Happy are the pure in heart: they will see God!

Happy are those who work for peace among men: God will call them his sons!

Happy are those who suffer persecution because they do what God requires: the Kingdom of heaven belongs to them!

MAKING RIGHT MY ATTITUDES

After each verse of Scripture, use one of the following symbols:

* If you understand the verse clearly
? If you have a question about the meaning
† If you get special inspiration from the verse
‡ If you really get convinced about something in your life

JAMES 1:2-5

2. My Brothers! Consider yourselves fortunate when all kinds of trials come your way. . . .

3. . . . for you know that when your faith succeeds in facing such trials, the result is the ability to endure.

4. But be sure that your endurance carries you all the way, without failing, so that you may be perfect and complete, lacking nothing.

5. But if any of you lacks wisdom, he should pray to God, who will give it to him; for God gives generously and graciously to all.

1. In all honesty, what is the greatest "trial" you are facing at the moment?

2. What alternatives do you have for dealing with the problem?

3. Do you feel that you can trust the others in your small group to help you in dealing with the situation?

EVALUATING MY RELATIONSHIPS

PHASE ONE

1. Murder is defined in the Scripture passage as (circle one):
   (a) killing your brother
   (b) slandering your brother to others
   (c) tearing down your brother's self-worth
   (d) making it difficult for your brother
   (e) not giving in to your brother

2. According to the passage, God expects (circle one):
   (a) the person who has done wrong to go to God and make it right
   (b) the person who has been wronged to go to God and make it right
   (c) the person who has done wrong to go to the person and make it right
   (d) the person who has been wronged to go to the person and make it right

3. Jot down in the space below the names of the people with whom you live at the moment. Then beside each name, place one of the following symbols.

○ Our relationship is completely affirming. I build up this person and he builds me up. We enable each other to be our best selves.

◐ Our relationship is half affirming. I try to build up this person but he refuses to build me up.

◑ Our relationship is half affirming in the other direction. This person tries to build me up, but I do not know how to build him up.

● Our relationship is mutually destructive. I tear down this person's self-worth and he tears down my self-worth. We are destroying each other.

_____   _____

_____   _____

_____   _____

PHASE TWO

1. Since starting in this small group, I think I have started (circle one):
   (a) to believe in my own unique worth and special gifts
   (b) to accept some of my own weaknesses and faults
   (c) to trust God for my problems
   (d) to celebrate life in a new way
   (e) none of these
   (f) all of these

2. The kind of person who helps me to come out of my shell and be myself is (list three adjectives):

3. The area in my life where I have made the least progress lately is (finish the sentence):

MATTHEW 5:21-24

You have heard that men were told in the past, "Do not murder; anyone who commits murder will be brought before the judge." But now I tell you: whoever is angry with his brother will be brought before the judge; whoever calls his brother "You good-for-nothing!" will be brought before the Council; and whoever calls his brother a worthless fool will be in danger of going to the fire of hell. So if you are about to offer your gift to God at the altar and there you remember that your brother has something against you, leave your gift there in front of the altar and go at once to make peace with your brother; then come back and offer your gift to God.

MAKING RIGHT MY RELATIONSHIPS

After each verse of Scripture, use one of the following symbols:

* If you understand the verse clearly
? If you have a question about the meaning
† If you get special inspiration from the verse
‡ If you really get convinced about something in your life

I PETER 3:8-12

8. *To conclude: you must all have the same thoughts and the same feelings; love one another as brothers, and be kind and humble with one another.*
9. *Do not back evil with evil, or cursing with cursing; instead pay back with a blessing, for a blessing is what God promised to give you when he called you.*
10. *Whoever wants to enjoy life and have happy days must no longer speak evil, and must stop telling lies.*
11. *He must turn away from evil and do good, he must seek peace and pursue it.*
12. *For the Lord keeps his eyes on the righteous and always listens to their prayers; but he turns against those who do evil.*

1. Which verse in the Scripture passage is going to be the hardest for you to live by?

2. Since starting this retreat, which area in your spiritual life has seen the greatest growth? The least growth?

3. From your observation, where has been the greatest growth in the life of the person on your right? What about the person on your left?

EVALUATING MY LIFE-STYLE

PHASE ONE

1. The thing I feel Jesus was teaching in the Scripture passage is that (circle one):
   (a) my life-style is unimportant as long as it is founded on the rock
   (b) the only way you can know if your life-style is right is to see it in a "storm!"
   (c) you can avoid tragedy by building soundly in the first place
   (d) storms are good because they wash away life-styles that are unsound

2. The word "rock" in this passage refers to (circle one):
   (a) Jesus Christ
   (b) the Church
   (c) Scripture
   (d) the inner life in a person

3. In my own spiritual experience, the closest I have come to going through "bad weather" like the storm described in the Scripture passage was (finish the sentence)

4. The thing that sustained me through this stormy period in my life was (finish the sentence)

5. I find that the statement by Sam Shoemaker—see bottom—(circle one):
   (a) describes me exactly
   (b) leaves me cold
   (c) causes me to think
   (d) describes my former life-style.

PHASE TWO   Finish the following sentences:
1. The high point in this retreat for me has been:

2. The greatest thing I have learned from this retreat is:

3. If I knew that I could count on the support of my group, the thing I would give myself to in the future would be:

"The inner life of many people is simply vacant. They may have once had a faith to give life coherence and meaning, but the widespread materialism around them and the corrosions of secularistic philosophy in education have robbed them of it. So we fill our hands and our time with all kinds of activity to make us forget, while our souls are empty of those convictions and standards which alone give life purpose and direction. People turn to pleasure, business, radio and television, sex, drink, drugs—anything to fill the emptiness within"—Sam Shoemaker.

MATTHEW 7:24-27   *So then, everyone who hears these words of mine and obeys them will be like a wise man who built his house on the rock. The rain poured down, the rivers flooded over, and the winds blew hard against that house. But it did not fall, because it had been built on the rock. Everyone who hears these words of mine and does not obey them will be like a foolish man who built his house on the sand. The rain poured down, the rivers flooded over, the winds blew hard against that house, and it fell. What a terrible fall that was!*

MAKING RIGHT MY LIFE-STYLE

After each Scripture passage, mark one of the following symbols:

* If you understand the verse clearly
? If you have a question about the meaning
† If you get special inspiration from the verse
‡ If you really get convinced about something in your life

I CORINTHIANS 9:24-27   24. *Surely you know that in a race all the runners take part* *in it, but only one of them wins the prize. Run, then, in such a way as to win the prize.*

25. Every athlete in training submits to strict discipline; he does so in order to be crowned with a wreath that will not last; but we do it for one that will last forever.

26. That is why I run straight for the finish line; that is why I am like a boxer, who does not waste his punches.

27. I harden my body with blows and bring it under complete control, to keep from being rejected myself after having called others to the contest.

1. Using the same analogy that Paul used in the Scripture passage, how would you compare your spiritual-training discipline to Paul's?

2. What has been the greatest achievement in the retreat as far as your spiritual life is concerned?

3. If you had a chance to belong to another group like this, would you do it?

4. What is the greatest wish you have for each person in your group?

EVALUATION

This retreat was designed for sophomore, junior, and senior high school students. It proved to be a very effective model. It was intended to be a concentrated weekend program, providing opportunities for personal growth, spiritual encounters, and group interaction. This may seem like a difficult task in such a short time span. Time can be an asset, as well as a liability. Some exercises may be especially important for a group. The leader should check with the director if that group wishes to continue while other groups move ahead with the schedule. Or, one could come back to the exercise during free time. The retreat is at least a beginning for some to examine their life-styles. Response will be varied. The full impact of the retreat may come later for some. Don't anticipate results.

Do not keep a strict eye on the clock for beginning/ending exercises. Be flexible. Don't be afraid to exercise options in the schedule.

Something that cannot be given over-emphasis for this model is the bringing together of different groups. The interaction of familiar and unfamiliar is an important part of group process. Invite another parish, youth group, CCD class to the retreat. If possible, they should help in the planning of the retreat and provide additional staff members.

Size of the group will vary. Eighty to a hundred was found to be effective for this age level. If possible, divide into groups of seven to ten for discussions, exercises, etc. Try to choose group leaders carefully. They are very important to the group. Do not expect each group to establish an immediate sense of community, trust, sharing, etc. Some groups will have to work at this more than others. (Group leaders may need to initiate optional games or exercises such as Praise Bombardment, Brown Bag or direct confrontation such as: I feel we are not being honest here. How do you feel? Or go around the circle. *Each person* must tell exactly how he feels about every *other member* in the group. Go around the circle again; let each person respond.)

If participants are allowed to stay up all night, expect to find things getting off to a slow start in the morning. It may be necessary to set a curfew for Friday night and none for Saturday night as Sunday's schedule is lighter. With careful planning and organizing, this will not be just another retreat, a weekend encounter, rap session, or sensitivity program. It will be a searching, a sharing, and caring. It will be an experience in living.

IDEAS FOR FOLLOWING UP THE PROGRAM

There are several ways of following up on the retreat model. Some suggestions are made here. One will be able to initiate others, designed for a particular group.

1. If it is a CCD group or youth group, much of the retreat material could serve as a basis for subsequent classes or meetings (e.g., the valuing process, relationships, group games, and films).

2. One may want to get together as a group for a Scripture and/or social service using some ideas presented at the retreat. (Show some of the films again. Young people are psyched for re-runs and they may get more out of them a second time.)

3. A note to priests. How about using some of the ideas on beatitudes, relationships, person of Jesus, etc., as themes for future homilies.

4. If you use packets or folders for each person, they can refer to the themes, exercises, etc., at later intervals. Go through some of the same exercises. Note how some answers, opinions, values have changed/have not changed.

5. Send out questionnaires at a later date, asking participants to re-evaluate the retreat. Note any new thoughts or ideas.

6. Provide an opportunity for group to get together for a social function—picnic, swimming, hayride, etc. Now that they've experienced a retreat weekend, how about a weekend trip? Take time out for Scripture, liturgy, rap sessions, etc.

RESOURCE BOOKS

The approach to this retreat is based on *Values and Teaching*, by Sidney Simon. The content relies heavily on two Serendipity Books, *Rap* and *Breaking Free*, by Lyman Coleman. Because of their importance, these three books are listed separately. Additional books listed below, have been very helpful in planning retreats, group discussions, talks, etc.

Breaking Free (1971)
Lyman Coleman
Word, Incorporated—Waco, Texas

Rap (1972)
Lyman Coleman
Word, Incorporated—Waco, Texas

Values and Teaching (1966)
Sidney Simon, Louis Raths, Merrill Harman
Charles Merrill Publishing Company—Columbus, Ohio

Sacramental Experiences (1970)
Margaret Linane
Majestic Publishing Company, Inc.—Woodland, California

Healing and Forgiveness (1967)
Alfred Longley
World Library Publications, Inc.—Cincinnati, Ohio

Self-Awareness Through Group Dynamics (1970)
Richard Reichert
George Pflaum, Publisher—Dayton, Ohio

Carl Rogers on Encounter Groups (1970)
Carl Rogers
Harper & Row Publishers—New York, New York

Discovery Series
Paulist Press—Paramus, New Jersey

The Giving Tree (1971)
Shel Silverstein
Harper & Row Publishers—New York, New York

Xpand (1970)
Richard Reichert
Ave Maria Press—Notre Dame, Indiana

Group Discussion as Learning Process (1972)
Elizabeth Flynn and John LaFaso
Paulist Press—Paramus, New Jersey

Kaleidoscope, Serendipity, Coffee House Itch (These are all
    Serendipity Books)
Lyman Coleman
Word, Incorporated—Waco, Texas

II. TEEN—MODERN:
A VARSITY FOOTBALL TEAM RETREAT

by Rev. Ken Keifer, O.F.M.

A. THEME/PARTICIPANTS

INTRODUCTION

Young people frequently have moral values imposed from the outside by parents, priests, teachers, and so on. The internalization of such values is essential if the youngster is going to develop into a Christian with high moral standards. Even with such internalizing, there is a definite need to reinforce these moral values from time to time. During the retreat, we attempt to learn what moral values the retreatants have adopted, if any. We challenge their position, their opinions, and moral view, for the sake of clarification and reinforcement. In discussions, the retreatants are forced by pure questioning to define and defend their values. This naturally leads to personal growth and development, not only in the area of religious values, but indeed in the area of human development as well. Through discussion with their peers, team building is also effected. During this retreat with the football team we tried to build *a team before the players ever hit the field.* It was our goal to get individuals who, in some instances, did not really know each other to get to know each other well, to develop friendships with one another, so that when the football season started, they would indeed know one another, be able to relate to one another and, therefore, be able to play together as a team in a much more effective way.

DESCRIPTION OF THE AUDIENCE

This model can be used mainly with junior and senior students from a large Catholic high school. This retreat could be used with any similar group whose values are not clear, whose positions on faith and morals are somewhat shaky. The audience was made up mainly of teenagers, therefore, young people who had already begun to question the teaching of the Catholic Church, who are not sold on the positions that are presented to them by their religion teachers. In the group, however, we did find some solidly established Christian values; we found that there were Catholics who had a great love for the Eucharist, and for the liturgy, for the teachings of the Church, and on the other side of the spectrum, we found individuals who questioned almost everything. It was our attempt and our goal to take the students where they were at and not where we would like them to be. We tried to relate the material to football situations. We did not attempt to water down the Catholic faith, but we tried to help the students grow and develop from the positions where they found themselves.

In dealing with high school students—there were 58 high school boys together with eight football coaches—we tried to work not only with them, but with the coaches as well. We felt that if we could tie them together so that they would work as a team, this team would serve as a model for the high school student to imitate. We encouraged the leaders, the coaches, to participate in all of the activities, and they served as an example.

B. OUTLINE/SCHEDULE

1. RETREAT SCHEDULE

Varsity Football Team Retreat

The program presented below was designed for a group of high school students who were "trying out" for the varsity football team.

GOAL Reinforcement of moral values.
Personal development.
Team-Building through group dynamics.

SETTING Time: Monday evening thru Thursday afternoon.
Place: CYO Retreat House, Cleveland.
Circumstances: In-fighting among previous varsity players had demoralizing effect on team. Coach wanted to begin season on spiritual tone. Attendance was compulsory, and not accepted by all, including some assistant coaches.

MATERIALS NEEDED 1. Pencils and paper.
2. Area large enough for eight small groups.
3. Eight tables large enough to accommodate each group.

SCHEDULE **First Evening**
Briefing session for coaches. Individual goal setting for coaches: "What do you personally expect from praying, working and playing with the football players during the next four days?"

Sessions on First Day
11:00 a.m. *Introduction*
Within each small group, mention their names and answer the question: "What three things would you like people to remember about you?"

Discussion: Reflections on points made by group members. Check to see if everyone knows each other's name.

12:00 p.m. Lunch
1:30 *Football Team Crisis*
Goal: (1) Group Interaction.
(2) Clarification of values.

Technique: A detailed description of this technique together with other pertinent information may be found in *A Handbook of Structured Experiences for Human Relations Training*, Vol. III, p. 108 (University Associates Press, P.O. Box 615, Iowa City, Iowa 52240).

Setting: Sub-groups consisting of eight members are formed. Everyone is briefed on the "facts" of the crisis. Each group is given a definite role to play—e.g., one group is "the faculty," another, the "alumni club," etc. As discussions progress, further information is given to certain groups.

5:00	Liturgy: Theme: "I have a dream."
6:00	Supper
7:30	Talk by member of campus crusaders for Christ.

Theme: How I found Christ. Speakers are available in most large cities thru the diocesan CYO office.

9:00-10:30   Recreation

During this time each coach has a private conference with members of his group to check on each football player's personal progress up to this point.

11:00	Retire
11:15	Briefing session with coaches on progress.

Sessions on Second Day

9:30 a.m.   *Introduction*

New groups are formed. A member in each group describes his best friend without mentioning his or her name. After each has had his turn, members are asked to respond "yes" or "no" to the following question: "Do you think you will be able to find a person such as your best friend within this group?"

10:00   Inclusion—Clarifying values

Each member is asked to select five players out of ten who they feel would work well as team members. A brief description of each player is presented and individuals must make a decision on that information. Once each person has selected five players, the sub-group strives to reach a consensus or a choice of five.

11:00   *Dyadic—Encounter*

A description of this technique may be found in *A Handbook of Structured Experiences for Human Relations Training*, Vol. I, p. 97 (University Associates Press, P.O. Box 615, Iowa City, Iowa 52240).

1:00-2:30 p.m.   Recreation—Group Activities

2:30   Movie—Discussion

"Right Here, Right Now!"

This film deals with what one person can do in accepting others and including them in the group. It can be obtained from

> Public Relations Office
> 3140 Meramec Street
> St. Louis, Missouri 63118

4:00	Dyadic encounter with another member of the group
5:00	Liturgy
7:30	*Open Session*
	Coaches and team formed a large circle. The head coach began the session by giving his impression of group and individual progress. Feedback and observations on group and individual behavior were invited.
9:30	*Group Recreation*
	Because of the tension created by the open session, all participants were required to take part in the recreation. Coaches made it a point to give positive reinforcement to group members evaluated during the open session.

Sessions on Third Day

9:30 a.m.	*Introduction*
	In light of what you have experienced during these sessions, make a *team motto*.
	New sub-groups were formed and each group discussed a motto and the reasons behind its choice. When a decision is reached, sub-groups join in an attempt to reach consensus.
11:00	*Win as Much as You Can*
	Procedure and application of this technique may be found in *A Handbook of Structured Experiences for Human Relations Training*, Vol. 2, p. 66.
12:00 p.m.	Dinner
1:30	Wrap-up session
1:30	Clean-Up and departure

2. OUTLINE OF THE CONTENT OF EACH PROJECT

"What do you personally expect from praying, working, and playing with the football players during these next four days?" In the first sessions with the coaches we tried to establish personal goals and objectives.

11:00 a.m. Introduction—We wanted each student to get to know the others better so that they could work more effectively as a team. We asked this question—What three things would you like people to remember about you? It was our intention here to develop the student's self-image and his self-confidence so that each student would get to know one another a little better.

1:30 p.m. Football Team Crisis—We established a crisis within a high school where a student was caught cheating, that is, two students were caught cheating. Both were on the football team, and as a result of their cheating, they were being dropped from the team just before a very important game. In this crisis situation we broke up into small groups, with each group role-playing one of the school's groups. Each group was given a definite role to play. One group, for example, was the faculty, another the alumni club. They were to resolve this crisis, and in so doing they would express their values—how they felt about studies, about cheating, about the relationship between studies and the spiritual life.

5:00 Liturgy: Theme—I Have a Dream was based on the words of Dr. Martin Luther King. Through the liturgy we tried to say that there are dreamers and dreamers—in the sense that some men have dreams that they build on good, solid foundations, such as Dr. King, John F. Kennedy, and Robert Kennedy, and there are other people who have dreams of destruction and of despair such as Lee Harvey Oswald, James Earl Ray and Sirhan Sirhan.

7:30 Talk—Talk by a campus crusader for Christ—"How I Found Christ." He was an outstanding athlete at the high school prior to entering into college and at college he also was a noted sportsman. The purpose of his talk was to try to give the students an ideal that they could imitate, and to show them how they could relate sports and their religion in one harmonious unit.

9:00-10:30 Recreation—During this time each coach would call in a team member that he had had in his group all day and talk to the student to ask him if the day had been profitable and if he had noticed any growth and development. He would try to help the student grow spiritually and in a human way during the next day.

11:15 Briefing Session with the Coaches—Here again we tried to review the entire day and tried to find out how we could structure the next day so that it would be more profitable for all.

Second Day 9:30 a.m.—On this day we again divided into new groups and again the purpose was to help the students to get to know one another better. This time we asked the group members to describe their best friend without mentioning his or her name. They were also asked whether or not they could find such a friend in this particular group of 58 football players. The goal of the exercise was to help them to develop new friendships in this group.

10:00 Inclusion—The purpose of this particular exercise was to clarify values—to have the players review the good qualities and the bad qualities of ten potential team players. They were to discuss the good points and the bad points of having these individuals on the team. In this way they would clarify their own position, their own values—what they expected to see in others on the team and what members of the group with whom they were having the discussion expected of them.

11:00 Dyadic Encounter—This encounter consists of 40 questions taken from the *Handbook of Structured Experiences for Human Relations Training.* Here you give a student (students are divided into pairs) the set of 40 questions. When he finishes the first five, he gives the paper of questions to his partner and the partner then asks the first five questions. When they finish the first five, they switch papers again, and the first man asks his partner the questions from six to ten. When he has completed these questions he returns the paper to the partner who has just answered the questions and that partner now asks the first individual to complete the following sentences: We have found this most rewarding—; it really plays a great part in deepening friendships—; students really get to know each other in a meaningful way—.

2:30 p.m. Movie Discussion—"Right Here, Right Now"— tells briefly in a graphic way what one individual can do in order to tie many people together into one solid unit. This movie is from the public relations office at 3140 Merimac Street, St. Louis, Missouri. It tells how one man, coming into an apartment where a great variety of people live, through his concern and his understanding, made friends with everybody in the apartment and was able to help them with their personal problems.

4:00 Dyadic Encounter—This takes place with a new individual so that each football player gets to know several individuals in depth during the few days of the retreat.

7:30 Open Session—We tried to bring into the open some of the difficulties that we were experiencing within the group—individuals again forming into little cliques, individuals not being free and open with one another—in general, a clearing of the air in which the coaches tried to point out what they had noticed occurring within the group during the past two days. Feedback and observations on the group and individual behavior were invited. This was followed by group recreation, because the previous session had caused a certain amount of tension. It was good because we felt that it was one of the highlights of the retreat—students could really express their opinions openly with one another.

Third Day 9:30 a.m.—Again we broke up into small groups, again with new members in each group. And this time we asked the football players to come up with a team motto. Each group developed its own motto. Through a consensus we began putting one group with another. Eventually the entire football staff put together one motto that has since become the motto of the team.

11:00 "Win as Much as You Can"—The purpose of this game is to show that we should not operate as individuals, but as a team. When we operate as a team we accomplish much more. Divide the students into groups of eight; pair off the students— four pairs of two. Each partner is to decide whether he is going to choose x or y, and depending on what the entire group does, he either wins or loses so many dollars. If they play together as a team, win as much as they can, "they" being interpreted as all eight players, then they are going to come out very successfully. But if they play as individuals or partners they are not going to do as well.

1:30 p.m. Wrap-Up Session—We encouraged ten students

to put into practice the various things they had learned during the past three days. It was a closing-off session—an attempt to bring together all of the loose ends and to give the football players and the staff the encouragement they needed to go out and develop a good team.

C. GUIDELINES

1. ADMINISTRATIVE PROCEDURE

One day before the program started we met with group leaders and discussed their goals and expectations. Then we went over the entire program with the group leaders and played some of the games ahead of time.

Need for Direction for Each Project

Goal—help students clarify their religious values, get to know one another better and build up a team spirit.

Forming groups—pull name out of hat. Each day put students into new group. Although the good facilitator doesn't participate a good deal, he would have to interject ideas, ask questions and help clarify.

First Day Introduction—A group leader is at each table and he explains to the participants that they are to mention three things that they would like people to remember about them. It's a good idea for the facilitator to start himself by mentioning his name, where he is from, and three things that he would like the group members to remember about him. Then go around the circle so that everyone makes a contribution. Ask for reflections. Encourage open communication.

Football Team Crisis—The director of the program reads in a very dramatic way the facts of the crisis so as to stir up interest and enthusiasm with the entire group. He tries to make this as lively and pertinent as possible. Before he makes his presentation, however, the students again are divided into small groups—again using random or formal appointment of individuals to a particular group. After he has made his presentation, the director then advises the facilitators at each table to pass out additional fact sheets to each participant at that particular table. This additional fact sheet tells the members at a particular table what role they are supposed to play. The facilitator must make sure that the individuals in his group understand clearly the roles that they are to play. The second fact sheet is different for each participating group. One group does not know what the other group has on its second fact sheet. From time to time the director of the group gives input of new situations developing. Since the director does not know what or how the general group is going to solve the problem, he tries to get both groups to sit down to argue out the crisis themselves and arrive at a position on which they can agree. Then he goes on to the other groups trying to get two to agree on a position. When this is accomplished, he tries to combine four groups, finally putting the whole group together so that they might arrive at one opinion or point of view. The entire process takes two to three hours. When a consensus is reached by the individual group, those playing the faculty call a general assembly to have each group present its position.

During the above session people are to remain seated at the proper table with only a negotiator going from table to table.

9:00 a.m.—Recreation—During this time there is a briefing session with the coaches and feedback on how things are going.

9:30—Introduction—Again new groups are formed at random or by deliberate choice of the director and the facilitator. The facilitator begins by describing his or her best friend without mentioning his or her name. Then he asks each group member in turn to describe his best friend, always without mentioning names. After everyone has done this, the question is asked: "Do you think you will be able to find a person such as your friend within this group?"

When each group participant has responded to this question the facilitator may ask further questions concerning why each feels that he will or will not meet such an individual within this group. There may be a certain amount of embarrassment in this procedure, so the facilitator should be very keen to the feelings of people within his group and should try to keep the conversation going as well as he can.

10:00 Inclusion—The directions are as follows:

Each member is given a sheet labeled "inclusion." He is asked to select five members that he would like to see on his particular football team. Each member listed on the inclusion sheet has good and bad qualities, and the participant is forced to make a decision: He is going to have to rethink his values—what he likes to see in a player and what he does not like to see. Each participant is asked to select the five players privately as an individual. When each participant has made his choice, the entire group of eight or ten participants, depending on the size of the group, is asked to reach a consensus of what five players they as a group would like to select and put on the team. Each individual, therefore, is going to have to make known his choices to the facilitator or to other members of the group. They are going to try to see, first of all, where they agree and where they disagree. Immediately they will select those on whom there is a general agreement. Then they must discuss back and forth the pros and cons of why they should or should not select this particular individual. When each group has selected its five members to join the football team, a general assembly is called, the attention of all the groups is called. The director then asks each group to mention the five players that it has selected to go on the football team. This, too, may lead to a general discussion of why one player was selected in preference to another. The discussion should be open so that each individual can express his opinion and his views. It is also possible that after this discussion each group will reach a consensus so that all of the participants will agree on the five players who should be admitted to the team.

11:00 Dyadic Encounter—Individual team members are now paired off, at random or again by deliberate choice on the part of the director and the facilitators. Chairs are placed around the room so that participant A is looking directly at participant B. The chairs should be separated far enough apart so that partners do not interfere with the conversation of other partners. The arrangement of the room, therefore, should be thus:

In one corner you have A looking at B.

In the middle of the room you have C and D facing each other.

In the far corner of the room you have E and F, and so on, until you have all the participants paired off.

Again, try to make sure that pairs are far enough separated from other pairs so that their conversations are not overheard.

When the participants have taken their places, the facilitator states that each participant will be given a set of questions and will ask his partner five questions, sentences that need completion. When he is finished with the first five questions, he will give his partner the booklet and the partner, beginning with question 1, starts the encounter over again. The director should inform all of the participants that the data discussed will be kept strictly confidential. They should not look ahead in the booklet or in the pages which contain the questions. Each partner responds to each statement before continuing. The statements are to be completed in the order in which they appear. Don't skip any. Of course, a participant may decline to answer any question asked by his partner. He should stop when his partner is becoming obviously uncomfortable or anxious. Partner A begins by asking partner B to complete this sentence: "My name is"—to which B responds by giving his name. Then A asks question 2: "I live at"—and B responds by giving his address. A continues to ask the first five questions. When he is finished, he gives the booklet to B who begins again by asking A to respond to the following sentence: "My name is"—and A answers by giving his name. B repeats question 2: "I live at"—and A gives the address where he lives. B continues asking A the questions until he has come to number 5. When he is finished with number 5, he returns the booklet to A and A continues by asking B questions 6 to 10. When B has responded to these questions, A gives him the booklet and B now asks A the same questions until all of the questions have been covered alternately.

Dyadic Encounter at 4:00 p.m.—This is conducted the same way as earlier in the day. However, different partners are selected in order that participants get to know each other and a variety of people in a more meaningful way.

Open Session at 7:30—A large circle is formed in which the coaches are spaced at various intervals throughout the entire group. The head coach begins the session by giving his impressions of the group and of individual progress. Then he asks for feedback from individuals or from other group members. Since this is an open session, and since it can become, if you will, a sensitivity session, the director must be very alert to what is going on in the entire group. He must keep it moving so that it does not zero-in on any individual in great depth. Such an individual might feel as if the entire group were picking on him. If statements are made which may have hurt the feelings of individuals within the group, at the end of this particular session the facilitator must make sure that he talks to these individuals. In actuality, this was really not such a dangerous or sensitive point, because with football coaches nearing the season of football practice, we felt rather confident that in the open discussion the coaches would be reacting to individuals in the same way that they would be in the future on the football team. In practice, coaches are very open in evaluating the plays and performance of the individual players and so, in a sense, this was a preview of coming attractions. The coaches felt free to give feedback to individual participants, who, in turn, felt free enough to express their views and opinions to the facilitators and the coaches. The group recreation at 9:30 in the evening was very important.

2. MOTTO MAKING

The group is divided into sub-groups consisting of eight members. Each group is given the task to make a motto that will remind it of experiences during the retreat and inspire it to continue to grow.

When the first two groups have completed the task, have them form one group and, through consensus, formulate one motto, using their original motto as a starting point. Have the next two groups do the same. Keep joining the sub-groups until the entire group is back together again with one motto which expresses the ideas of the smaller groups.

We suggest that artists within the group print the motto on a large piece of cardboard and place it in the locker room so that group members will be continually reminded of their one goal.

MATERIALS NEEDED
Paper and pencils.
Tables and chairs so that small groups have room to work.
A large piece of cardboard.
Crayons or watercolors or Magic Markers.

PURPOSE
To reinforce values.
To promote group interaction.
To teach consensus-reaching.
To provide means for continued reinforcement.

We found that this technique worked very successfully. The motto became the pride of the football team and was printed in the local newspaper as a reason for their good team spirit.

3. WIN AS MUCH AS YOU CAN

PURPOSE
To teach team-building.
To promote group-interaction.
To reinforce value of cooperation.

GROUP SIZE
Unlimited number of octets. Each group of eight members is sub-divided into four partnerships. Each set of partners faces the other, sitting about six feet apart.

TIME REQUIRED
A minimum of thirty minutes.

MATERIALS NEEDED
"Win as Much as You Can" tally sheet for each player.
Pencils.

PHYSICAL ARRANGEMENT
Chairs are arranged according to the directions of a compass: two chairs, side by side, in a northernly position, two to the east, two to the south and two to the west. They are placed in such a way that partners are facing each other. The distance between one set of partners and another is about six feet.

PROCESS
1. Partnerships are formed and the participants are told to take their places.
2. Participants are told the name of the game and asked to keep the goal in mind during the game.
3. They are reminded that they may not talk to anyone but their partners during each round, except the fifth, the eighth and the tenth. This includes non-verbal communications also.
4. One minute is the time allotted for rounds 2, 3, 4, 6, 7, and 9. Two minutes are given for the first round. For rounds 5, 8, and 10, three minutes are allowed for a group discussion, then, one minute for partners to confer with each other before making a decision.
5. For rounds 5, 8, and 10, the four partners in one group pull their chairs together and discuss the way that the group should vote. However, they do not make their decision at this time. They discuss a course of action for three minutes as a group. Then, the partners return to their places and discuss their own personal view on selecting x or y. At a signal from the facilitator, each partnership writes down its decision.
6. After each decision is written down, the partnerships announce their decision to the others in the group. They then mark down how much they won or lost, depending on the decision of each partnership in the group.
7. When all ten rounds are completed, the facilitator opens up a

discussion on the interpretation of *you* in "Win as Much as You Can." By collaborating, groups could win more than by acting in a competitive spirit.

8. If time permits, the facilitator may want to discuss how to make life situations win-win experiences, rather than win-lose or even lose-lose situations.

4. WRAP-UP SESSION

PURPOSE

To reinforce values experienced during the retreat.
To inspire the participants to action.

TIME

Approximately one hour.

PHYSICAL SETTING

Have participants and facilitators sit around in a large circle. Facilitators should mix in with the participants to show solidarity.

PROCESS

The director asks: "What event made the biggest impression upon you during the past few days?"

He starts with a participant who is known for making responses in perspective and goes around the circle from there.

When each has had a turn, the director summarizes the main points made by the group and encourages them to continue this team spirit and concern for one another back at school.

We found that this is a meaningful experience for participants and greatly supports individual team members. It is a fitting conclusion for a team-building retreat.

D. TALKS/EXERCISES

1. FOOTBALL TEAM CRISIS

Fact Sheet

WEDNESDAY

9:00 a.m. Mr. Marshall, a senior math teacher, gave his students their quarterly exam. The test covered most of the material to date since Mr. Marshall was dissatisfied with the class performance.

9:35 Mr. Marshall caught Bob Leary and Frank Corowitz, two borderline students, cheating on the examination. He gave them each a failing grade which made them scholastically ineligible to play football, effective 3:00 p.m. Saturday. Leary played quarterback on the varsity team for two years, and Corowitz was a star offensive lineman.

1:15 p.m. Leary and Corowitz had a conference with Mr. Marshall. They told him that Saturday's game was crucial toward winning the championship and asked him not to have them dropped from the team. Mr. Marshall, however, told them that honesty and a good education were more important than sports. He refused to change his decision.

2:45 Coach Martin was informed that Leary and Corowitz had just become scholastically ineligible to play football. Following school policy, the coach sent a memo to the students telling them that they would not be able to play in Saturday's game.

3:15 About a third of the students held a protest rally outside Mr. Marshall's office.

Time Unknown Team members, angered over the action, met secretly to plan a course of action.

THURSDAY

8:30 a.m. In a surprise move, the president of the Alumni Club called on the principal. The editor of the Paduan attempted to get a statement from the two men when they emerged from the conference, but was greeted with coldness. The editor said later that it was evident that Mr. Murphy, the president, was very upset.

10:45 The Student Council president requested a meeting with the principal. The principal said that he would be glad to meet with him or any representative of the council. A time for the meeting was to be announced later in the day.

WIN AS MUCH AS YOU CAN

Directions: For ten successive rounds you and your partner will choose either an "X" or a "Y". The "pay-off" for each round is dependent upon the pattern of choices made in your cluster:

4 X's: Lose $1.00 each

3 X's: Win $1.00 each
1 Y : Lose $3.00

2 X's: Win $2.00 each
2 Y's: Lose $2.00 each

1 X : Win $3.00
3 Y's: Lose $1.00 each

4 Y's: Win $1.00 each

Strategy: You are to confer with your partner on each round and make a *joint decision*. Before rounds 5, 8, and 10 you may confer with the other pairs in your cluster.

STRATEGY

ROUND	TIME ALLOWED	CONFER WITH	CHOICE	$ WON	$ LOST	$ BALANCE
1	2 mins.	partner				
2	1 min.	partner				
3	1 min.	partner				
4	1 min.	partner				
5	3 mins.	cluster				Bonus round: pay-off, multiply by 3
6	1 min.	partner				
7	1 min.	partner				
8	3 mins.	cluster				Bonus round: pay-off, multiply by 5
9	1 min.	partner				
10	3 mins.	cluster				Bonus round: pay-off, multiply by 10

(Adapted from Gellerman)

2. BASKETBALL VARSITY PLAYERS

You are members of the Padua Basketball Varsity, meeting

together to decide what to do or say when a representative from your group meets with the principal tomorrow. Besides the material on the fact sheet, you have the following information:

1. If Leary and Corowitz are officially declared "scholastically ineligible" for football, they will not be able to play for the basketball varsity either. Corowitz was the second highest scoring man on the varsity.

2. Without Leary and Corowitz the team has little chance of going to the state finals.

3. Pat Foster, a varsity member who could not be present, called earlier and said he had heard that the two football players had deliberately flunked the math exam as a test case. Leary and Corowitz were "convinced that they could force the principal to back down and let them play."

3. ATHLETIC BOOSTER CLUB

You are members of the Athletic Booster Club, meeting to decide on a plan of action to present to the principal when a representative from your group meets with him tomorrow. You are angry at Leary and Corowitz because you have worked so hard for the team. Besides the fact sheet, you have the following information:

1. Mike Zoco, a member of the club, telephoned to say that Corowitz was out "partying it up" the night before the exam.

2. John Parks, the publicity chairman, has made a great effort to get a large crowd to attend Saturday's game. It is rumored that presidential candidate George McGovern, who will be in town, may make an appearance at the game.

3. It is the general feeling among Booster members that Leary and Corowitz deliberately put the team in a bind by failing their exams.

4. ALUMNI CLUB

You are members of the Alumni Club, meeting to decide on a plan of action to present to the principal when a representative from your group meets with him tomorrow. You are angry at Leary and Corowitz because you have worked so hard for the team. Besides the fact sheet, you have the following information:

1. Mike Zoco, a member of the club, telephoned to say that Corowitz was out "partying it up" the night before the exam.

2. John Parks, the publicity chairman, has made a great effort to get a large crowd to attend Saturday's game. It is rumored that presidential candidate George McGovern, who will be in town, may make an appearance at the game.

3. It is the general feeling among Alumni members that Leary and Corowitz deliberately put the team in a bind by failing their exams.

5. CLASSMATES

You are fellow classmates of Leary and Corowitz and are meeting to discuss what you might do to win Saturday's game. Besides the fact sheet, you have the following information:

1. Leary and Corowitz often and publicly have ridiculed the coach's "stupid rules."

2. Tony Viccaro, a classmate who is absent today because of illness, told another classmate that he heard the two football players say that they were going to flunk the math exam and force the principal to change the ineligibility rule.

3. Leary and Corowitz's girl friends are very upset because of the math teacher's action.

6. FOOTBALL TEAM

You are members of the football team, meeting to draw up your position to present to the principal. You know the school regulations; they're quite clear. However, you feel that Leary and Corowitz are essential for the success of Saturday's game. The question you face is this: "Do you consider scholastic excellence important enough to run the risk of losing Saturday's game?" Besides the fact sheet, you have the following information:

1. Leary and Corowitz were never too interested in studies.

2. Coach Martin, in a special announcement, reminded all team members of the school policy on scholastics ineligibility and told them to study hard for the quarterly exams.

3. There is a strong rumor going around that Leary is going to be offered a football scholarship to Notre Dame.

7. STUDENT COUNCIL

You are members of the Student Council, who are meeting to work out a plan of action to present to the principal tomorrow when a representative of your group meets with him. Besides the fact sheet, you have the following information:

1. Leary and Corowitz sought offices on the Student Council but both were defeated. Now, they ridicule and look down on Student Council members.

2. There is a rumor going around that friends of the two football players are trying to organize a protest demonstration.

3. The official "ineligibility list" has not been published so there is hope that the principal and faculty will listen to a reasonable proposal.

8. *STUDENTS AT PADUA*

You are fellow students of Leary and Corowitz and are meeting to discuss what you might do to win Saturday's game. Besides the fact sheet, you have the following information:

1. Leary and Corowitz often and publicly have ridiculed the coach's "stupid rules."

2. Tony Viccaro, a classmate who is absent today because of illness, told another classmate that he heard the two football players say that they were going to flunk the math exam and force the principal to change the ineligibility rule.

3. Leary and Corowitz's girl friends are very upset because of the math teacher's action.

9. *FACULTY*

You are members of the faculty, meeting in the home of Harry Jackson, another senior math teacher. You are meeting to formulate a statement that you can present to the principal and the student body. While you demand scholastic excellence of your students, you feel that sports also play a major role in high school life. Besides the fact sheet, you have the following information:

1. Leary and Corowitz have been borderline students since they began playing sports two years ago. However, they both have high IQ's.

2. There is a strong rumor that Leary may be given a football scholarship to Notre Dame. If he is dropped from the team this year, he probably will not get the scholarship.

3. Mr. Jones reported that other high schools in town are watching to see how you resolve this difficulty. He said that if you don't take a strong stand, other students will follow Leary and Corowitz's example.

TO: Athletic Booster Club
     Padua High School

Thursday night

Gentlemen:

I heard a rumor to the effect that you were planning on taking my son, Robert Leary, "out to the woodshed" and "giving him a good beating." If you so much as lay a hand on him, I will have you all arrested! I can't believe my son would "cheat." Besides, it's a family affair.

SENT BY: Charles Leary

10. INPUT TO FACULTY

To: The Principal
From: Mr. Marshall

I wish to make my position clear. I have worked hard to be a good teacher—often staying after school to help students who were having difficulty. Prior to our recent Quarterly Examination, I told the class that the test would be essential to their getting a passing grade. Bob Leary and Frank Corowitz just sneered at my warning.

If you fail to take action in the case of Leary and Corowitz, you will have serious trouble trying to inforce any regulation.

Sincerely,

H. Treston Marshall

11. MEMO TO ALL STUDENT GROUPS

Memo to All Student Groups, i.e., Student Council
Class 519
Padua Football Squad

From: Bill Moriarity, President, Student Council

It has been brought to my attention that Bob Leary and Frank Corowitz used gross and profane language while talking to Mr. Marshall. There is also a strong rumor—and I emphasize "rumor" —that these two players are not serious about the practice of their religion and make insulting remarks about the Church in general.

While this is merely "hearsay," I ask you to seriously consider what type of players we want representing our school. Only when you answer that question can you reasonably decide what course of action you wish to take in the case of these two players.

I hope to meet with a representative from each student group in the near future.

Sincerely,

Bill Moriarity

12. OFFICE OF THE COACH

From: Coach Martin

To: Padua Football Squad

Again and again I have told you that a good moral life is essential for any football player who represents our school.

Over and over I have stressed that each player must learn how to fulfill his responsibilities to his studies and the team.

If you people can't resolve these questions, I will submit my resignation and there'll be no football this season. I can't train irresponsible players.

Coach Martin

13. INCLUSION

You have been appointed co-captain of the football team. The coach has asked you to advise him on making the final cuts. Only five of the following men trying out for the team can be put on the roster:

(1) A player who was dismissed from the team last year for stealing in the locker room. Recommended by the Booster Club as a very direct and forceful personality who knows his will.

(2) A mediocre player whose father attends all the practices and is very friendly with an assistant coach. This student also has a great team spirit.

(3) A popular student who has a strong desire to get on the team because he wants to show the coach and the players "how to win the crown." He has been accused of being a "showboat" by many of the teachers.

(4) A transfer student who tackled last year's quarterback and put him out of action for the rest of the season. He has worked hard in practice, shown good talent in football, but is not too popular with the other players.

(5) A student who shows a great deal of potential as a football player, but who consistently disregards training rules.

(6) The president of the Student Council who has never played high school football but shows some signs of developing into a good punter. Because of conflicting duties, he will have to miss many practice sessions.

(7) A player whose father has promised to "treat the team to a steak dinner after its fifth victory." This student has skill in playing football, but is always afraid of being hurt during practice and games.

(8) A player who is very interested in getting a football scholarship to the U. of Cincinnati. He has already contacted the university to send out scouts to observe him and has asked the coach to send films of every game to the university.

(9) A player recommended by the girls of Nazareth. He is a mediocre player, but would present a good image for the school. Should he make the team, the school would receive strong backing from Nazareth.

(10) A student who has a terrific school spirit and who has sold $400.00 in ads for the athletic program. He tries hard and will be crushed if he doesn't make the team.

14. PERSONAL INFORMATION EXCHANGE

Reference: *HANDBOOK OF STRUCTURED EXPERIENCES FOR HUMAN RELATIONS TRAINING,* Pfeiffer and Jones.

All the data discussed should be kept strictly confidential.

Each partner responds to each statement before continuing.

The statements are to be completed in the order in which they appear. Don't skip items.

You may decline to answer any question asked by your partner.

Stop when either partner is becoming obviously uncomfortable or anxious. Go on to the next item. Either partner can stop the exchange.

In order to make sure that the information conveyed by the first speaker is being correctly understood, the second speaker (listener) should occasionally repeat *in his or her own words* what the first speaker has just said. The first speaker must be satisfied that he has been heard correclty.

Look up. If your partner has finished reading, turn the page of the booklet and begin. Please speak quietly enough so that you do not disturb groups nearby.

1. My name is . . .

2. I live at . . .

3. The reason I'm here is . . .

4. Right now I'm feeling . . .

5. When I think about the future, I see myself . . .

6. When I am in a new group I . . .

7. When I enter a room full of people I usually feel . . .

8. When I am feeling anxious in a new situation I usually . . .

9. In groups I feel most comfortable when the leader is . . .

10. Social norms make me feel . . .

11. I am happiest when . . .

12. The thing that turns me on the most is . . .

13. Right now I'm feeling . . .
    (Look your partner in the eyes while you respond to this item.)

14. The thing that concerns me the most when I meet a new person is . . .

15. When I am rejected I usually . . .

16. To me, belonging is . . .

17. A forceful leader makes me feel . . .

18. Breaking rules that seem arbitrary makes me feel . . .

19. I like to be just a follower when . . .

20. The thing that turns me off the most is . . .

21. I feel most affectionate when . . .

22. Toward you right now I feel . . .
    (Look your partner in the eye when you answer this.)

23. When I am alone I usually . . .

24. In crowds I . . .

25. In a group I usually get most involved when . . .

26. To me, taking orders from another person . . .

27. I am rebellious when . . .

28. Have a two or three minute discussion about this experience so far. Keep eye contact as much as you can, and try to cover the following points:
    How well have you been listening?
    How open and honest have you been?
    How eager are you to continue this interchange?
    Do you feel that you are getting to know
    each other?

29. The emotion I find most difficult to control is . . .

30. My most frequent daydreams are about . . .

31. My weakest point is . . .

32. I love . . .

33. I feel jealous about . . .

34. Right now I'm feeling . . .

35. I am afraid of . . .

36. I believe in . . .

37. I am most ashamed of . . .

38. Right now I am most reluctant to discuss . . .

39. Interracial dating and/or marriage make me feel . . .

40. Right now this experience is making me feel . . .

41. The thing I like best about you is . . .

42. I want you to . . .

E. MATERIALS/RESOURCES

MATERIALS NEEDED

A chalk board or an easel with a large pad of paper and Magic Markers. Paper and pencils should be available for every participant. In regard to mimeographed material, the football-team-crisis fact sheet should be mimeographed so that there is one copy for every participant.

When you break up into small groups, each member of the small group should have an additional fact sheet in accordance with the role that his particular group is playing. For example: You should have approximately eight copies of the Basketball Varsity Players' fact sheet, eight of the Athletic Booster Club fact sheet, eight copies for the group playing the Alumni Club role, eight copies for the group members who are playing the role of class-mates, eight copies for those who are playing the role of football team members. For the students who are forming the Student Council, each participant should have a copy of the Student Council fact sheets. Those playing the role of students at Padua should have a copy for each member, namely, eight copies. There should be a copy for each person playing the role of a faculty member.

In regard to the input, you will need one copy of each segment of input.

The exercise labeled "inclusion" should likewise be duplicated so that each member of the entire group has a copy.

In addition, when you break up into small groups there should be one copy per small group so that each small group might arrive at a consensus.

In regard to the dyadic encounter, each page, which contains 41 questions in all, should be duplicated so that there are enough copies for half of the total group. The reason for this is that once an individual has gone through the questions, the other individual using the same sheets repeats the same questions.

The game "Win as Much as You Can" should be duplicated so that each pair of participants has before him an outline of how to play the game. Since there are eight participants in each cluster, you should have four copies per cluster.

F.   LITURGIES/HOMILIES

ON BEING A DREAMER

"Happy the Man"

Happy the man who wanders with the Lord,
Happy the man who knows how to live,
Happy the man who never seeks reward,
Giving because he loves to give.
He seeks no gold,
He wants no gain,
He knows those things are all in vain.
He needs no praise nor honor too.
His only motto: "To your own self be true."
Happy the man who learned how to pray,
Happy the man who has a burning goal,
Happy the man whose service needs no pay,
This man has found his own soul.
Happy the man,
Happy the man, of the Lord.
            Sebastian Temple

PRAYER   Joseph the Dreamer (Genesis 37:5-20)

SCRIPTURAL   *Leader:*   "You are like salt for all mankind. But if salt loses its taste,
RESPONSE   there is no way to make it salty again. It has become
                        worthless; so it is thrown away and people walk on it"
                        (Matthew 5:13).

            All: "Unless you remain in me you cannot bear fruit, just as a
                        branch cannot bear fruit unless it remains on the vine"
                        (John 15:4).

            Leader: "You are like light for the whole world. A city built on a
                        hill cannot be hid. Nobody lights a lamp to put it under a
                        bowl; instead he puts it on the lamp-stand, where it gives
                        light for everyone in the house" (Matthew 5:14).

            All: "In the same way your light must shine before people, so
                        that they will see the good things you do and give praise
                        to your Father in heaven" (Matthew 5:16).

The Vision of Christ (Matthew 26:62-66)

Homily and Meditation

Prayer for Leadership (Peace Prayer of Saint Francis)

ON BEING A DREAMER

Make me a channel of your peace
Where there is hatred
Let me bring your love
Where there is injury
Your pardon, Lord
And where there's doubt
True faith in you.

Make me a channel of your peace
Where there's despair in life
Let me bring hope
Where there is darkness—only light
And where there's sadness—ever joy.

Oh, Master, grant that I may never seek
So much to be consoled as to console
To be understood as to understand
To be loved, as to love, with all my soul.

III. TEEN AND YOUNG ADULT—MODERN: A VALUE CLARIFICATION APPROACH

by Charles Bloss, O.F.M.

A.   THEME/PARTICIPANTS

TEEN AND YOUNG ADULT—MODERN:
A VALUE CLARIFICATION APPROACH

THE THEME OF THE MODEL AND THE AUDIENCE:

This model attempts to deal with issues that are of concern for teenagers and young adults, i.e., those of high school and college age. It is an effort to help the young adult focus on concerns and personal values such as: identity—identity confusion; intimacy—isolation; trust—mistrust; autonomy—shame and doubt; etc. (confer Erik Erikson's epigenetic chart on the stages and crises of human development in *CHILDHOOD AND SOCIETY*, chapter 7; and *IDENTITY: YOUTH AND CRISIS*, chapter 3). This model attempts to create a situation in which the young adult can personally reflect on his or her values in a non-threatening climate in which he or she is free to share this personal reflection with others, or free not to share. The goal is to help the person come to a clearer realization of the precise values that are presently reflected in his or her life.

The leader who uses this model, or any similar one, is advised to be well acquainted with the literature and resource material available in the field of value clarification. The enclosed bibliography should be consulted. Also, previous experience using value clarification techniques and strategies is helpful. Resource persons familiar with these techniques should be tapped, along with the reading resources in this field. If the leader is unfamiliar with the use of this approach, it could become just a series of interesting exercises. Reading in the field and experience will safeguard against this danger.

B. OUTLINE/SCHEDULE AND GUIDELINES

1. OUTLINE OF THE CONTENT

**A Modern Retreat for Teenagers and Young Adults:
A Value Clarification Approach**

The Theme of the Model and the Audience
A Proposed Time Schedule
An Expanded Outline for Leader and Staff
An Outline of Content and Directions

2. A PROPOSED TIME SCHEDULE

This schedule is for a proposed two-day retreat. It comprises six sessions, with 26 possible exercises.

Evening: 7:00 p.m.-9:00 p.m., *Session I* (Orientation and Personal Identity)

Morning: 8:00 a.m.-9:00 a.m., breakfast
9:00-12:00, *Session II* with break (Clarification of Personal Values)
12:00 p.m., lunch
12:30-3:00, free time
3:00-6:00, *Session III* (possible liturgy—Personal Values and Change)
6:00, dinner
7:00-9:00, *Session IV* (Interpersonal Dimensions of Personal Values)

Morning: 8:00 a.m.-9:00 a.m., breakfast
9:00-12:00, *Session V* with break (Religious Values; or Just Values)
12:00 p.m., lunch
1:00-3:00, *Session VI* (closing liturgy—Back-Home Application)

3. *EXPANDED OUTLINE FOR LEADER AND STAFF*

Session I—Orientation and Personal Identity

Orientation
Exercise 1: "Why I Am Here" Fantasy (15-20 minutes)
Exercise 2: "I Am" List (30 minutes)
Exercise 3: Personal Focus (30 minutes)
Exercise 4: Film (optional)

Session II—Clarification of Personal Values

Lecturette on Values (10 minutes)
Exercise 1: Word Association (10 minutes)
Exercise 2: Agree-Disagree Statements (10 minutes)
Exercise 3: "Love" List (15 minutes)
Exercise 4: Value Sheet (30 minutes)
Exercise 5: Rank Ordering (15 minutes)
Exercise 6: "Concern" List (15 minutes)
Exercise 7: Coat of Arms (15-30 minutes)

Session III—Personal Values and Change

Exercise 1: Value Sheet (15-30 minutes)
Exercise 2: Film: "Is It Always Right To Be Right?" (30-60 minutes)
Exercise 3: Sentence Completion (30-60 minutes)
Exercise 4: Living Continuum (15-30 minutes)

Session IV—Interpersonal Dimensions of Personal Values

Exercise 1: Identity Search (1-1½ hours)
Exercise 2: How I See Myself (15-30 minutes)
Exercise 3: Value Sheet (30-60 minutes)
Exercise 4: Discussion (optional)

Session V—Religious Values—or Just Values

Exercise 1: Personal and Gospel Values (45 minutes)
Exercise 2: Religious Value Scale (1 hour)
Exercise 3: Value Sheet (45 minutes)

Session VI—Back Home Application

Exercise 1: Review of Objectives (15 minutes)
Exercise 2: Write Yourself a Letter (15 minutes)
Exercise 3: Staff Feedback (10 minutes)
Exercise 4: Closing Liturgy

NOTE: The above time notations are merely approximations. In some cases, they do not include sharing time, which is indeed essential. After making their own adaptations, the leader and staff will again want to make their own tentative timetable for each session. It is good to provide a short *break during the longer sessions.*

C. TALKS/EXERCISES

Session I—

(Orientation to physical surroundings; any "rules" to be followed; housekeeping details, when staff will be available for private chats, etc.).

THEME   An orientation to the purpose of a retreat, i.e., personal reflection, sharing, and growth as a person. Stress should be put on the fact that the retreat is not the staff or retreat master's responsibility primarily, but that of *each person* involved in the retreat. Personal gains will be in proportion to personal investment and involvement. The theme of this first session is to review why and how each person came to the retreat (group fantasy), how each person sees himself or herself at present ("I Am" List), and what each person hopes to get out of this retreat, (written privately and shared with group). It should be emphasized to the participants of the retreat that in *all* the personal reflections and exercises each person is totally free to share with the group only those reflections that he feels comfortable sharing. But also, it should be noted that the risk of personal sharing, initiative and involvement with other members of the group will result in the greatest degree of personal learning experience, insight and growth.

MATERIALS NEEDED   A large room, preferably with a rug, in which participants can spread out on the floor with enough free room around each, tables for writing on, notebooks and pencils for each, Scotch or masking tape or pins, a blackboard or newsprint board with masking tape, the option of a film screen and projector for Exercise 4 and possible use of a question box.

DIRECTIONS   *Exercise 1*—"Why I Am Here" fantasy: Have the participants spread out on the floor, lying down with room between each. Lighting should be dim while the leader creates an atmosphere of quiet and reflection. The leader asks all to relax, closing their eyes if they wish, and begins to take the group on a fantasy trip as to how each came to be here now. Have the participants get in touch with an awareness of themselves, become aware of their breathing, take deep breaths, become aware of their pulses, of their own present feelings, points of physical discomfort as they are on the floor. Then say: "Think back to when you first heard about the retreat. From whom did you hear about it? What was your first reaction—one of anticipation, indifference? When did you make the decision to come to the retreat? At that time, what were you hoping to get out of it? Think about your immediate preparations—getting packed, saying goodbye, the trip here, your first reactions and response to this place. Who was the first person you met when you arrived here? What did you do, talk about, think about during your first interactions here? Right now, what are your personal goals and hopes for this retreat? How do you plan to work to realize these goals?"

The purpose of this exercise is to focus the participants' awareness on the here-and-now situation and the sessions ahead —to leave all their past plans, worries, concerns, etc., at home, and make the most of the retreat. It is an exercise for personal focusing and not for sharing with others. It usually takes about fifteen or twenty minutes. The leader's role is of utmost importance in establishing an atmosphere of quiet reflection and "slowing down" the rapid, often unreflective pace that prevails in our everyday lives. The leader should move the group through the fantasy at a leisurely, informal pace, *pausing* sufficiently after each suggested idea to provide time for the participants' rumination.

Exercise 2—"I Am" List: First, have the participants write the numbers 1 to 10 in their notebooks; then instruct them to complete each number with—e.g., "I am a grouchy person in the morning," "I am confused," "I am self-confident," "I am afraid of what others say sometimes," etc. Give a *minimum* of instructions for this exercise. It should be sufficient for you to tell them to complete the "I am" sentence in any way they wish, ten times. When they have had enough time to complete the ten, have them tape or pin the list on their chests and walk around the room *in silence* quietly reading each other's lists. Silence at this point may be difficult to maintain, but it is of great value for this portion of the exercise. After sufficient time, tell them that they may now mill around and talk briefly with anyone, to share further, ask questions, etc. This exercise is particularly good for members who do not know each other. It breaks the ice on a personal level. For that reason, it may also prove to be somewhat threatening to some. You may want to announce at the time they begin to make their lists that they will be silently sharing their lists. This exercise ordinarily takes about 30 minutes.

Exercise 3—Personal focus on this retreat: Have the participants take their notebooks and write a paragraph discussing what they personally hope to gain from this retreat. Urge them to be as specific as possible in their writing. Stress that what is written in each notebook is the personal, private property of each person and is not to be read by another without permission. This notebook is their personal diary for their reflections during and outside of retreat sessions. After sufficient time has been given to complete this paragraph, the leader opens the group for a general discussion of the specific interests and concerns that they want to deal with during the retreat. The leader uses a chalk board or newsprint chart to list the issues voiced. Participants are free to state what they wrote in their diaries, or spontaneous suggestions and interests. After all have had an opportunity to state their opinions, the leader tapes the newsprint on the wall (or keeps the blackboard visible in a prominent place) for all to reflect on throughout the remainder of the retreat. This list will be returned during the final session. The purpose of this public discussion is to get the input from those involved, to make their needs plainly visible, to provide the staff with areas to focus upon during other sessions and discussions during the course of the retreat. The following sessions should take into account as much as possible this public listing of purposes. This may necessitate some revision and refocusing of material already prepared for the following sessions. The exercise takes about 30 minutes.

Exercise 4—If time remains, the leader may want to make use of a film to close the first evening. Some suggestions are offered with source materials at the end of this retreat.

PROCESS

The leader is a key person in establishing an atmosphere and climate of relaxed seriousness and genuine openness. He should be willing to model for the group the type of communication that he would like to see develop. Often the best use of the value clarifying materials is evident if the group can be broken down into units of six, eight or ten persons, with a leader (staff member) in each group. Those slow to verbalize in a large group speak more freely, and all have more "air time" to express themselves. While some may experience a degree of anxiety with value clarification procedures, the usual response is to get quickly involved because the process invites personal activity and reflection. Again, personal responsibility for the experience of the retreat rests with each person (continue to remind them of this). They "own" the content of these exercises and are encouraged, but never forced, to share this with the group. (If there is a liturgy planned for the next day, the leader may want to meet at the close of the first session with those interested in planning group participation in the liturgy.)

Session II—

THEME

The concern of this session is to help clarify personal and religious values. A number of value clarifying techniques are employed to this end. The examples given here, as throughout this retreat, are only suggestions as to possible content questions and statements. The more that the content is tailored to the needs and concerns of the participants the better. Leaders of the retreat are encouraged to meet beforehand, if at all possible, with representatives of the retreat group so that the content structuring of these exercises will speak to their specific needs and interests. The theme of this session is perhaps best expressed in the following lecturette which opens this session.

LECTURETTE

(This is a good place to again remind the participants that they are primarily responsible for what they get out of the retreat.)

The purpose of what we are going to do this morning is to try to clarify some of our own personal values. Albert Einstein has characterized our age as being one of "a perfection of means and a confusion of goals." Where do our values and goals come from? Sometimes we say that this or that is a value for us—but how do we really know? A value should have certain qualities about it. For example—1. It should be something that is *freely* chosen. 2. It should be chosen after examining the possible *alternatives*. 3. It should be chosen after thoughtful consideration of the *consequences* of each alternative. Moreover, a value should be something that we—4. *prize* and *cherish*; 5. we are willing to *publicly affirm*, to share with others and talk about. A value should be something that—6. we *act upon*; and 7. act *repeatedly* upon, so that patterns of behavior emerge from our values. A value should be something that our lives *celebrate* (cf. L. Raths' *VALUES AND TEACHING*, Hall and Smith's *VALUE CLARIFICATION AS LEARN-ING PROCESS*, and the sheet on "definition of values" enclosed).

Most assuredly, a listing of our *activities* tells us more about what we prize and cherish than any eloquent statement of our beliefs. Our jobs and our lives are not to be concerned with keeping a dreary watch over the ancient and medieval values of past generations, but to face squarely the grim but bracing task of *re-creating* those past values of history and civilization in our own lives. Values cannot be simply transmitted from one generation to the next, but only re-created in the personal lives of the living. Today we want to take a closer look at ourselves, to perhaps unfreeze some of our attitudes, to re-examine what we say are "our values." I am not going to tell you what is or should be a value for you, but rather help you reflect for yourself on what your values are at present. If I tell you that non-smoking, physical exercise, and letter writing are *values* for me, you wouldn't know for sure if they are or not. If you look at my actions and see that I continue to smoke, do not exercise, and seldom write letters, you would get a much clearer picture of the truth. Values are personal. I cannot impose my values on you—e.g., "Why don't you . . .?" Nor should I *depose* your values—e.g., "You really don't want to do. . . ." Values can only be *shared* with another—e.g., "This is the way I act. My reasons are. . . ." Thus, I must leave you free to accept or reject my values. Let us take a look at some of our values.

MATERIALS NEEDED

Notebooks and pencils, value sheet on leadership or another topic, content of exercises for leader.

DIRECTIONS

Exercise 1—Word Association: Have a list of words drawn up beforehand (e.g., prayer, Coke, Peace Corps, drugs, marriage, astronaut, God, war, etc.). Tell the participants to write in their notebooks the very first word they think of when you say the word "prayer." Use about 15 or 20 words, not all serious. Finish by having them share some of the words. This allows them to see concretely how they are all different and unique and establishes the legitimacy of being different. It gets the sharing process started on a non-threatening, fun level (about 10 minutes).

Exercise 2—Agree-Disagree Statements: Have the participants stand facing each other in a large circle. Give them a statement to which they can respond in a non-verbal way—e.g., "I was in favor of President Nixon's trip to China." They can respond in five non-verbal ways: 1. agree—arms outstretched and thumbs up, 2. disagree—arms outstretched and thumbs down, 3. agree strongly—arms outstretched and thumbs waved up in circular motion, 4. disagree strongly—thumbs down in a circular motion, and 5. pass—arms crossed. This again establishes the legitimacy of being different openly before each other. Examples of statements:

High school students do too much drinking today.
Things are changing too fast in the world today.
I am in favor of school busing to provide integrated schools.
Sex is exploited too much in advertising.
I am in favor of the women's lib movement.
I feel a little bit anxious right now.
More people should use Listerine in the morning.

The statements can be fun or serious. There should be some of each, and the leader will want to formulate the content in such a way as to get at concerns and interests of those involved (10 minutes). The statement: "I feel personally that drugs (or pre-marital sex) are OK"—can be more personally involving than "Someday I would like to get married."

Exercise 3—"Love" list: Have the participants make a list in their notebooks of at least ten things that they really love to do; the list can be longer. When they are finished:

Have them put a $ sign in front of each one that costs *more than* $3.00 every time they do it;

Put a 5 in front of items that would *not* have been on their lists five years ago;

Put a P in front of items that their parents did not do but would have enjoyed doing;

Put a minus sign in front of items that they are not willing to share right now with this group;

Put a date down for the last time that they did each of these items, etc.

Make up other questions of your own. Interpretation: If all of my "love" list activities cost me money, that tells me something of my values; if all the things I love to do are dated six months or a year ago as last done, that tells me something (15 minutes).

Exercise 4—Value Sheet: The topic of the value sheet can be anything that would be of interest to the participants. It should take a position on some issue, and the questions that follow should be related to explicit or implicit issues in the quotation. The questions should not be slanted to elicit a certain response as being "right." Confer with the enclosed value sheet on leadership.

Newspapers, school policies, books, etc., can be used to provide a statement, or write your own. The statement should be short and clear as to the opinion of the author. The questions should neither agree nor disagree with the position of the statement, but should broaden the issues in such a way as to focus on how this quote applies to similar decisions and questions facing those using this value sheet. After all have had ample time to complete the sheet privately, have them discuss this (and other exercises) in small groups (30 minutes). It is good to have a short break at some point during this long morning session.

Exercise 5—Rank Ordering: The leader uses the blackboard or newsprint to write a statement followed by three possible alternatives. The participants rank (1st, 2nd, 3rd) the alternatives according to their own personal preference, e.g.,

1. I would most like to be able to:
   —be as angry on the outside as I am on the inside
   —cry when I feel like it, but not at the drop of a hat
   —boldly ask for affection when I need it.

(After they have ranked them, give them the option of writing another response that they would most like to be able to do even *more* than any of those listed.)

2. I value my free time because:
   —it gives me a chance to catch up on what I'm behind in
   —I am able to get involved with others (family, etc.)
   —I enjoy time to be alone with myself.

3. My behavior is most influenced by:
   —the rules of those in authority over me
   —what my friends are doing
   —my own conscience.

Again, these are only given as possible examples. You can add many of your own with the particular focus you would like your participants to explore (15 minutes).

Exercise 6—"Concern" list: Although similar to the "Love" list, the focus here is on the future, i.e., things you are personally concerned about and would like to do something about before you die. Have the participants make a list of at least ten such concerns. Then ask them these (or similar) value clarifying questions:

1. Put a check mark by those concerns which you have actually discussed with others;
2. Put an asterisk by those which you have actually done something about within the last two months;
3. Put an x by those which other people could help you to accomplish;
4. Put a minus sign by those you have never done anything about;
5. Underline the two most important concerns on your list;
6. Circle the most important one of the two.

This exercise helps to separate our fantasies and dreams from what is actually reflected in our everyday life-style. These concerns can now be approached realistically and with some deliberate planning and goal setting (15 minutes).

Exercise 7—Coat of Arms: In the Middle Ages, and also today, families, societies, etc., used a coat of arms as a visible sign to represent what their values and lives were about. Have the participants take a large sheet of paper and draw a large shield or coat of arms, dividing it into six compartments. They are going to make their own personal coat of arms. On it they are to write nothing, but only draw symbols, pictures, etc.

1. In the first compartment, draw a picture or symbol of that which you do best.
2. The biggest success of this past year for you personally;
3. The biggest failure of this past year for you;
4. That which you just will not budge on (your most firmly held conviction);
5. If you just discovered that you have only one year to live and could do anything you wanted to with that year, how would you choose to spend that last year of your life?
6. You can write in the last compartment only three words. Write those you would choose to tell other people who you really are (like an epitaph).

This can be a very personal experience, and some may be reluctant to share with others what they put down. This is their privilege. Those, however, who would want to share this and past exercises with others in the group (or small groups) should have some time to do this. The sharing may take the rest of the morning, or another exercise can be used here. Ample opportunity should be provided to share personal values without anyone feeling that he is forced to do so. The leader will have to judge the amount of time to be spent on each exercise in relationship to the response and interest of the participants. A caution to be observed throughout: *go slowly* and allow plenty of time for personal reflections in each exercise. Much non-visible, personal activity will be taking place (15-30 minutes).

PROCESS   These exercises are fun to do and people get easily involved in them. They also contain much serious content and touch deeply personal values which may not be visibly apparent until the participants begin to share their reflections. The greatest benefit is derived when they share what they prize and cherish with others, always at their own pace. The leader's role in creating this climate of sharing is of utmost importance. If he is willing "to model," i.e., share his own values freely, the participants will readily respond. Small groups of six to ten, each with a staff member, are ideal. These groups for sharing can be fixed at random before the retreat, or mixed freely during each session. The normal response to these exercises is one of enthusiastic involvement.

Session III—

THEME

The theme of this session is change. What are our attitudes toward change, and how do we deal with it personally?

MATERIALS NEEDED

Value Sheet on Change, film, and accompanying value sheet, notebooks and pencils.

DIRECTIONS

Exercise 1—Value Sheet on Change (cf. *Session II, Exercise 4* for ways of making your own value sheets).

Exercise 2—Film—"Is It Always Right To Be Right?" narrated by Orson Welles. This excellent ten-minute film should be previewed before the retreat. There is an enclosed value sheet with divergent reactions to the film. After the participants have viewed the film and answered and discussed the value sheet, you may want to view the film again (30 minutes-1 hour).

Exercise 3—Sentence Completion: The following are some possible open-end sentences. You may want these mimeographed beforehand, or notebooks can be used.

1. When I think about my future. . . .
2. Right now in my life I am most concerned about. . . .
3. To me, being Christian (Jewish, etc.) means. . . .
4. If I were free to be myself, I would. . . .
5. If I were free to say what I thought about myself, I would say. . . .
6. If I could remove just one limitation from myself, I would. . . .
7. To be more understanding of others, I would need to. . . .
8. My strongest good quality is. . . .
9. The person who has most influenced my life is. . . .
10. He (she) has influenced me by. . . .

Add or substitute your own open-end sentences. Give sufficient time for reflecting upon and completing each sentence. Check to see whether or not the group would like to share with each other. Often they can be valuable resources to one another in understanding themselves (30 minutes-1 hour).

Exercise 4—Living Continuum: If you have time for this exercise, draw an imaginary line across the entire room, with one end being totally open to all possible change, the other end being totally closed to any change. Have the participants place themselves *physically* where they think they belong on the line, according to their own attitude toward change. Go through the line, giving each a chance to explain why he sees himself at that particular point on the line (15 minutes). (You may want to use this exercise immediately after *Exercise 1* or *2* above. You may want to have them list five times when they were right and five times when they were wrong. Or, have them list five persons they know who they consider to be open to change and why.)

PROCESS   As this is nearing mid-point in the retreat, energy levels may lag somewhat. The film is sure to grab the interest of the group. You may want to develop other value sheets from the many issues raised in the film. Also, you may want to interchange the order of the exercises. Again, the time spent on any given exercise should be determined by sensitivity to the group's response. You may want to consider some religious experience or liturgy before or after the session, or for the evening.

Session IV—

THEME   The theme of this session is an examination of personal values as they influence interpersonal relationships. The values we profess and practice may not always be shared by others. What happens when our values conflict with significant others in our lives? How do we handle conflict, authority, intimacy, and aggression in our lives? The exercises begin with a personal focus, then broaden to the interdependence of societies and nations on the issue of war.

MATERIALS NEEDED   Papers with the four alternative corners stapled together; list of statements for the leader; Value Sheet on War/Peace (enclosed) and Value Sheet on Rank Ordering: "How I See Myself."

DIRECTIONS   *Exercise 1*—Identity Search Exercise. The group assembles in the middle of a large room in which there are four different lists of alternatives taped to the wall, one list in each corner. The leader reads the first statement (e.g.—"What turns you on the most?") and instructs the participants to go to the corner which best fits them (e.g.—sports, food, opposite sex, music). In the corner they have chosen, they are to discuss with others in that corner why they see themselves where they are, how they feel in regard to their choice, what the strengths and weaknesses are of being there, etc. The leaders should mill around from corner to corner, facilitating the focus of the discussion. Some may have difficulty choosing any corner and may prefer to stay in the middle. They should be instructed to choose the corner that *best* fits them, although none may appear as entirely satisfactory to them. The discussion in the corners should proceed until the leader perceives that interest is waning; then he should move on to the next statement by having someone tear off the presently visible words, revealing the four possible alternatives for the next statement which he then reads. The participants then have a moment to decide which corner fits them, move to that corner, and share personal feelings about how it feels to be there. Participants should have their notebooks with them and jot down each corner they go to as they progress through the exercise. The words in each corner should be *boldly visible* from the middle of the room and stapled together so that, with the last page taped to the wall, previous words can be torn off as the exercise progresses. As another variation, if you have sufficient time, you may want to give each person an opportunity to express his (her) second (or *least* preferred) choice for each of the statements. This can best be determined by the responsiveness of the group members to this particular exercise, within your time limitations. The following are some possible statements you may care to use—or make your own (1-1½ hours).

1. What turns me on the most:
   sports—food—opposite sex—music
2. My place in my family is:
   only child—first born—last born—middle
3. The person I most identify with and turn to is:
   father—mother—peers—adult friend
4. The position I usually occupy in a new group is:
   wall-flower—dominating—wait and see—critical
5. My usual attitude toward conflict is:
   hawk—lamb—ostrich—chameleon
6. My basic attitude toward authority is:
   dependent—counter-dependent—alienated—indifferent
7. When others are angry with me my usual response is:
   feel hurt—withdraw—deny their anger—get angry myself
8. What I fear most about my future is:
   job possibilities—military service—failure in school—family conflict
9. As far as affection goes I:
   don't get enough—don't give enough—get more than I give—give more than I get

Exercise 2—How I See Myself—Rank Ordering: Have the enclosed value sheet mimeographed with copies for each person. Read through the sheet, then have them rank order (one to four) the way they see themselves as living most of the time. After they have written "me" in the left hand column and ranked themselves, have them also rank—1. the way *they see* their father (guardian) functioning most of the time; 2. the way they see their mother. They may want to discuss with each other what they have discovered (15-30 minutes).

Exercise 3—Value Sheet on War/Peace. This enclosed sheet is used as others above are (cf. *Session II, Exercise 4* above). You may want to precede this value sheet with a film such as "The Retreat," listed in the Resources.

Exercise 4—If time remains, you may want to—1. use some question box material for discussion; 2. use some issues listed on the board at the first session that have not yet been dealt with; 3. have an open discussion (perhaps optional) of their concerns; 4. spend some time planning the liturgy for the following day.

PROCESS   The identity search exercise should not become a party. It is relatively easy to decide upon a corner, but to focus the discussion in a meaningful way may encounter some resistance. It has value only if the participants are willing to take it seriously and honestly explore and share their reasons and feelings about being in the corner they go to. One of the dangers in most of the sessions is trying to pack too much into them. The amount of material and exercises employed should never be rushed through. It is far better to use one exercise well than to hurry through four as though they were lighthearted but personally remote games. The mood and atmosphere created by the leader are of critical importance to the use of any of the exercises.

Session V—

THEME   The last day begins with an effort to try to draw together and focus some of the values the participants have been exploring in previous sessions. The theme tries to focus on how their own personal values are related to those institutions in society that transmit religious values, e.g., churches.

MATERIALS NEEDED   Notebooks and pencils, Religious Value Scale sheets for all, Value Sheet on the Church.

DIRECTIONS   *Exercise 1*—Personal and Gospel Values: Have the participants again become aware that a retreat involves work, and explain the personal responsibility they share in reference to what they get out of it. Have them begin by spending about ten minutes making a list in their notebooks of what they consider at this point to be their own personal values. (Later, you may want to have them rank-order this list for themselves.) Next have them make a list of the values that they see Jesus Christ living by in the Gospels. Have them spend some time discussing how the two lists compare with each other. Time spent on this exercise will again be determined by the responsiveness of the group and their investment in it (45 minutes).

Exercise 2—Religious Value Scale: Using the enclosed scale, have the participants place an "x" on the continuum for each of the items, showing where they see themselves and their attitudes. Emphasize that they should have thought of specific and concrete reasons to explain why they placed the "x" where they did. After they have completed the scale privately, move through the list, giving all an opportunity to express where they see themselves and why. There are no "right" and "wrong" places to be. What is important, however, is *why* a person places himself where he does. All should have ample time to express their reasons in a non-judgmental atmosphere. This scale is very general and open-ended. You may want to focus on specific issues and questions behind these generic pole positions (1 hour).

Exercise 3—Value Sheet on Change in the Church (cf. *Ses-*

sion II, Exercise 4 above for the use of this or another value sheet you may care to make yourself).

PROCESS
One of the dangers with value clarification procedures is that they can, at times, remain too general and unfocused, and are consequently of limited value. Continue to remind the participants that they should try to be as *specific* and concrete as possible, both in the value they assume ownership for and the personal reasons behind it. Especially in *Exercises 1* and *2* above, emphasize the importance of being able to give *specific* reasons for their choices.

Session VI—

THEME
The effort of this session is to tie up any loose ends that may be dangling, and to focus on back home application of what has been learned during the retreat.

MATERIALS NEEDED
Black board or newsprint with stated objectives of the first session, stationery and envelopes for all, extra paper for feedback to staff.

DIRECTIONS
Exercise 1—Review of Objectives: Spend some time going through each of the interests and concerns that the group stated as their purpose during the first session. This group "objectives list" should be prominently displayed throughout the retreat. Now check out with the group how they feel about each interest or concern listed. Were they dealt with adequately? Spend some time dealing with issues that have not received proper attention. Remind them that they shared in being responsible for the achievement, or lack thereof, of these goals (15 minutes).

Exercise 2—Write Yourself a Letter: Give them a piece of stationery and an envelope. Have them write themselves a letter: 1. What I learned (or re-learned) on this retreat; 2. One specific project that I want to do something about. Have them specifically focus on one concern or aspect of their lives that they want to make a contract with themselves to do something about in the future. Have them think in terms of specific dates at which time they will re-evaluate their progress. This is the back-home application of what they learned from the retreat. 3. When finished writing, have them seal the letter in the envelope and address it to themselves. Tell them that the leader will mail these letters to them in three (six) months (15 minutes).

Exercise 3—Staff Feedback: Give participants a piece of paper and ask them to jot down their reactions: good and bad features of the retreat experience, things they particularly liked or disliked about the retreat. This exercise is for the benefit of the staff and leader to help improve future retreats. It is not necessary that they sign these comments (10 minutes).

Exercise 4—Closing Liturgy: You may want to close with some type of religious experience, prayer service, etc. If so, some group planning should have gone into it during the course of the retreat. It is often a very rewarding experience for both staff and participants to give the participants an opportunity to individually express what the retreat has meant to them. This can be done during the liturgy, or as a closing for this last exercise.

PROCESS

This session should be kept relatively short, as the participants are by now reorienting their lives and interests to the world they will be going back to. The letter to themselves is something that only they will ever see, and most will eagerly enjoy doing this. The opportunity to share what the retreat has meant to them should not be overlooked or minimized. It can be a very moving experience and something that binds them together for future activities that they may share as a group. The staff should meet after the retreat is over to reflect on the feedback they have received from the participants' comments. (It is quite helpful for the staff to meet periodically *during* the retreat to assess particular problem areas that may present themselves.)

All of the time allotments for the exercises are merely approximations. Sensitivity to the group's response will dictate the pace. Again, it is better to do fewer exercises well than to overload the systems of the participants with excessive content with which they cannot adequately deal. You may want to eliminate some of these exercises rather than overcrowd your schedule. Some could be thus used as follow-up exercises for the group at a later date. Also you can pick and choose from these exercises if your schedule is less than a two day retreat. Finally, these exercises are not intended to be taken as the best possible or only way of exploring values. Experimentation and variation are heartily encouraged.

SUMMARY—

The value clarifying approach can be a very exciting and creative endeavor. Those using it are urged to make their own adaptations of the above material and to create new exercises themselves. Because it engages people personally in the process of their own learning, it appeals to all ages and backgrounds. It is non-threatening because it operates on the assumption that values cannot be "taught"—they can only be shared, leaving the individual free to buy into that value or not. The process of clarification of personal values should *always* respect the right of the person to share or not to share his or her values. Nonetheless, the learning experience is enhanced to the extent that persons *are* willing to share what is of value to them. Ultimately, we "teach" values only if we ourselves are willing to share our values with others.

Young adults do much testing and searching as they explore the value systems they see around them. The value clarification approach helps them to focus more consciously, more directly, and more deliberately upon that process of exploration. Anyone working with young adults is well aware of the often vacillating and even contradictory ideas and behavior that they at times exhibit. Value clarification is an attempt to provide some tools with which to reflexively explore behavior. The resulting rewards are well worth the personal efforts of involvement.

Some today are concerned with the area of "religious" values. True values are reflected in our actions and patterns of living; it makes little difference what label we put on them; they are either values or not. In this sense, every value that we have is a religious value. And if we seek to communicate this or that religious value, we can only begin by sharing *how* it is of value *for us*. We cannot impose it on another for something imposed from the outside is never a true value to the one who receives it. A value is *freely* accepted, or not accepted at all.

D. MATERIALS/RESOURCES

1. BOOKS AND FILMS

BOOKS

Erikson, Erik. *CHILDHOOD AND SOCIETY.* New York, W. W. Norton & Co., 1963.

———. *IDENTITY: YOUTH AND CRISIS.* New York, W. W. Norton & Co., 1968.

Hall, Brian. *VALUE CLARIFICATION AS LEARNING PROCESS: A SOURCEBOOK.* New York, Paulist Press, 1973.

———. *VALUE CLARIFICATION AS LEARNING PROCESS: A GUIDEBOOK.* New York, Paulist Press, 1973.

Hall, Brian and Maury Smith. *VALUE CLARIFICATION AS LEARNING PROCESS: A HANDBOOK FOR CHRISTIAN EDUCATORS.* New York, Paulist Press, 1973.

Raths, L., M. Harmin, and S. Simon, *VALUES AND TEACHING.* Columbus, Ohio, Charles Merrill Publishing Co., 1966.

"Value Clarification" issue of *FORUM*, Spring/Summer 1972, published by the J. C. Penney Company, Inc., Educational Relations, 1301 Avenue of the Americas, New York, N.Y. 10019 (available to educators from J. C. Penney stores).

FILMS

"Is It Always Right To Be Right?" narrated by Orson Welles, written by Warren H. Schmidt, King Screen Productions, 320 Aurora Ave., N., Seattle, Washington 98109.

"The Retreat," Franciscan Communication Center, 1229 S. Santee St., Los Angeles, California 90015.

"The Eucharist," Franciscan Communication Center, 1229 S. Santee St., Los Angeles, California 90015. (This center has available catalogs listing its excellent films.)

2. A DEFINITION OF VALUES

REDEFINITION

In retrospect, then, we define a value as being the stance that the self takes to the world through the feelings, ideas, imagination, and behavior of the individual. The valuing process comes about through the free choice of the individual within a particular stage of his formation with its given limitations. And this choice must consider the consequences or the alternatives that are evident and must be, of course, a choice from alternatives. Essential to the valuing process also is that the choice must have been acted upon and becomes a permanent part of the life plan of the person if it is to be called a value. Finally, the person must be happy with the choice. It must be the one that enhances the development, emotional and spiritual, of that individual.

In order to clarify whether or not a given thing is a value or not, I should ask myself the following questions about it:

1. Was the value chosen from a range of alternatives of which I was aware?
2. Did I consider the consequences of those alternatives of which I was aware?
3. Is this value evident in my behavior? That is to say, have I acted on it recently?
4. Do I act on this value repeatedly in some fashion through a variety of similar experiences?
5. Am I happy and pleased with the choice?
6. Am I willing to state it publicly?
7. Does the value enhance, and not impede, the development of my emotional and spiritual well-being?

This is, of course, a slight modification of the Simon, Raths, and Harmin definition, but the criteria still stand. If I cannot answer yes to all of the above questions, then what I am speaking of is not a fully developed value. The next question that has to be asked is: How many chosen values, since the above is a chosen value, do we, in fact, live by? Is it possible that the majority of values that we have are part and parcel of our personalities and are assimilated through our upbringing? Would we choose the values of which we become aware? This whole question brings up the problem of the various types of values.

VALUE CLARIFICATION AS A LEARNING PROCESS: A SOURCE-BOOK, by Brian Hall. (Paulist Press, 1973).

SESSION II EXERCISE 4

3. LEADERSHIP

Leadership has always been an enigma in the world. Today's world sometimes appears to be "leaderless." Our present leaders seem afraid to lead. Perhaps each of us should just forget about them and be our own leaders—doing exactly what we want to do.

1. Do you agree with this statement? If not, what would you change to make it acceptable to you?

2. What are some appealing "styles of leadership"?

3. List five people who you consider to be leaders today.

4. How would you describe yourself as a leader?

5. List any specific activities in which you are involved as a leader. Are there any other activities in which you desire to become involved?

SESSION III EXERCISE 1

4. CHANGE

The first thing I think you must do as leaders in our community is to establish within yourselves a "formation to change" attitude, a "formation to accept change" attitude. Man by nature tends to be conservative, fearing the unknown and threatened by change. He can react to change in the Church, for example, in two ways—He can hide in his room, wring his hands and cry, "My God, what is happening to the Church?" He can bury his head ostrich-like in the ground, hoping that when he pulls it out the trouble will be all over and everything will be as in the past. It's not that simple and it seems to me that your job is to help people understand this.

1. Do you agree with the author's position? If not, what would you change to make this statement acceptable to you?

2. List those things which you feel should not be changed in the Church.

3. How would you describe the meaning of the word "change"?

4. What things would you like to see changed regarding yourself? List them, and then rank them in terms of their priority for you.

5. What are you willing to do *specifically to effect these changes?*

SESSION III EXERCISE 2

5. *IS IT ALWAYS RIGHT TO BE RIGHT?*

1. It takes courage to say: "I may be wrong. You may be right."
2. Two "rights" can make a costly wrong.
3. The value of learning, as well as teaching, listening as well as telling. (Influence must be a two-way process.)
4. The search for truth never ends
5. Social problems are solved not by one group blaming another, but by two groups reaching for understanding.
6. Our complex age requires the spirit of a "Declaration of Interdependence."
7. The film gives a good solution.

1. It is easy to admit a mistake.

2. Stand fast when you are right.

3. People must be obedient to teachers and leaders.

4. Truth is absolute, eternal, and unchanging.

5. We need strong leaders who can force people to act right

6. A man must learn to stand on his own two feet.

7. The film is too simplistic.

1. Choose the above statements with which you agree and explain why.

2. How do you feel and act when you are talking with someone whose views are quite different from your own? Write down an example.

3. How do you think another person feels when you disagree with him?

4. Make a list of useful "do's" and "don't's" to change an argument into a discussion where both persons can learn from their differences.

5. Why is it hard for some people to say: "I may be wrong"?

**SESSION IV
EXERCISE 2**

6. *HOW I SEE MYSELF*

Imagination—inspirational, creativity more important, search, process of developing and experimenting.

Function— —get the job done, operate chiefly from the point of view of use or accomplishment, emphasis on task-oriented relations.

Ideas — — —getting idea across is more important, intellectual approach, understanding entire process is basic.

Feelings — —feelings are more important than getting job done; where individuals are within a program or project, persons and feelings are seen as important as to how a task develops.

(Leader's directions: Have the participants rank: 1. "How do I see myself?" (rank 1-4); 4. "How do I see my mother?"; 3. "How do I see my father?" Place a "Me" at the top of the left hand margin and rank self, one through four. Do the same for the others. Rank deceased parents also.)

(This exercise is called the "Hallmark Card Game," reprinted from *Value Clarification as Learning Process: A Resource Book*, Section II, by Brian P. Hall and Maury Smith, Paulist Press, New York, N.Y., 1973.)

**SESSION IV
EXERCISE 3**

7. *VALUE SHEET ON WAR/PEACE*

The January, 1972 issue of the Washington Newsletter of the Friends Committee on National Legislation reports on a study of the world's arms trade conducted by Stockholm's International Peace Research Institute that was released in November, 1971. The study concludes that "the United States is the largest supplier of military equipment in the world, accounting for nearly half the world's total trade in weapons." We must now squarely face the fact that war is no longer tolerable for Christians. We must speak out loudly and clearly, and repudiate war as an instrument of national policy (from an editorial in *AMERICA*, February 19, 1972, and Bishop C. T. Dozier's Pastoral Letter, December, 1971).

1. Do you agree with the above statement? If not, change the statement so that you can agree. Explain why you agree or disagree.

2. Give your definition or description of a "peacemaker":

3. List five ways in which you have been a peacemaker:

4. List five living people you consider to be peacemakers:

5. List five new ways that you could be a peacemaker:

SECTION V
EXERCISE 2

8. RELIGIOUS VALUE SCALE

1. I am:

Sinner	Saved
Creature	Co-creator
Needing law	Needing Freedom

2. Others are:

Occasions of sin	Occasions of salvation
Bad	Good
Destined to fall	Trustworthy

3. God:

Just	Merciful
Remote	Present
Mysterious	Known
Spoke in past	Speaks now
One	Three

4. Church:

Protective	Open
Infallible	Fallible
Needs authority	Needs to serve

Roman Catholic											Broader
Shows self in dogma											Shows self in deeds
Hierarchy and Pope											People
Unchangeable											Changeable

5. The World:

Domain of evil											Kingdom of God
Where sin is											Where salvation is
Where living must be blessed											Where living is blessed
Static											Progressing to perfection
Captured in original sin											Seized by original redemption

6. Christ:

God											Man
Unlike me											Like me
Crucified											Risen
Completed His work											Still active

7. Salvation:

| Dependent on my needs | | | | | | | | | | | Gift of God through Christ |
| To be earned | | | | | | | | | | | To be celebrated |

8. Religion:

| God moral behavior | | | | | | | | | | | Worship of a lover |
| Is concerned with spiritual issues | | | | | | | | | | | Is concerned with worldly issues |

(This Religious Values Scale is adapted from Brian P. Hall's "The Psychology of Change," in *St. Anthony Messenger*, Vol. 77, (March 1970),p. 12-13.)

SESSION V
EXERCISE 4

9. VALUE SHEET: CHANGE IN THE CHURCH

Frustration over change in the Church occurs when inner-directed persons find that they are required to submit to the law "on the books." Extreme reactions to frustration will not do away with those who need the law "on the books." Christian sensitivity to the needs of others will require that the externally directed be served. Can it be possible, in our society, that while inner-directed persons are increasing, the majority are still externally directed? If so, meeting their needs sets up a pattern of priorities—1. they must be loved and not harmed; 2. they must be helped to inner directedness; 3. they must be seen as individuals who are a part of the people of God and therefore must be loved and helped in a way that promotes the common good. Finally, after they are able to direct themselves, the "law" can be generalized or taken from the books completely. This would appear to be a specific response to the Christian imperative to love our brothers (James F. Campbell in *THE PRIEST,* February, 1972).

1. Do you agree with the above statement? If not, change it so that it becomes acceptable to you.

2. Are you primarily an inner-directed or outer-directed person? List five examples indicating this:

3. List the pros and cons of being "inner-directed" and then of being "outer-directed."

4. List those changes which have taken place too fast for you in the Church:

5. List those changes which you think are taking place too slowly:

MY COAT-OF-ARMS

1. What you do best.

4. Something I will not budge on.

2. Your biggest success. (Past Year)

5. I have one year to live. What am I going to do?

3. Your biggest failure. (Past Year)

6. Three words that describe who I am.

PART TWO: MISCELLANEOUS RESOURCES

I. MODEL PENANCE SERVICES

TALKS/EXERCISES

Session I—Communal Penance Service

Priest: In the name of the Father, and of the Son, and of the Holy Spirit.

All: Amen.

Priest: Let us pray:
Our Father, we place ourselves before you knowing well that we have all done wrong, in the evil we have done, and in the good that we have not troubled to do.
You ask us only to do to your other children, to our brothers, what we would like them to do to us; but we, small and selfish, do to them only what gets us what we like. Together let us look at ourselves as we are and ask God's help to do better. This we ask through Christ our Lord.

All: Amen.

All: Father, we come before you knowing that we have fallen, and you tell us to stand up and walk. We cannot change the past, for what is done, is done; but today and tomorrow is your call to us.
Support us, Father, and hold us up with a full sense of how forgiving you are so that we may avoid the final wrong of refusing to take you at your Word.
Your Word of forgiveness to us, Father, is terribly serious; it took sweat, and nails, and blood—the body and life of your own Son—for you to say to each of us: "I forgive you, and I love you." For this we are ever filled with thanks, and will do our best to make our thanks real in the way we live in days to come.

Reading: Sirach 17:19-27.

Examination of conscience: (kneel)

Priest: For failing to remember that we ourselves and all we have are your gifts to us,

All: Lord, forgive us.

Priest: For failing to pray because we had other things to do that seemed more important,

All: Lord, forgive us.

Priest: For failing to respect our parents and all others whose love makes them care for us,

All: Lord, forgive us.

Priest: For being angry and deliberately trying to hurt others who are also your children, our brothers,

All:	Lord, forgive us.
Priest:	For taking what does not belong to us, or for being tight-fisted and selfish with what we have,
All:	Lord, forgive us.
Priest:	For speaking unkindly of others without care for their feelings, and for using the gift of speech to cause pain,
All:	Lord, forgive us.
Priest:	For being jealous of others, and unthankful for the many gifts you have given each of us,
All:	Lord, forgive us.
Priest:	For being afraid to stand up for what we know is right,
All:	Lord, forgive us.
Priest:	For not going out of our way to help others because we might be hurt or because it was too much trouble,
All:	Lord, forgive us.

(Other failings of our community may be added here.)
A pause for individual examination of conscience will follow.
After this pause we will recite the act of contrition.

Session II—Prayer of Confession and Examination

And so I confess before the Father who created us, who sustains us and who loves us so wonderfully; before the Son who saved us and who reconciles us to the Father, to ourselves and to each other; before the Spirit whose workings burn within us and unites us into one body;

I confess before all the saints, living and dead, who have found their happiness in the oneness of the personhood of Christ; before every ideal I have tried to attain and now find myself so short of; and finally I confess to you, brothers, who inspire me, who support me, who cheer me, that I have taken gifts that were given to me to be given to you, and simply refused to give them at all.

In every place that I have failed is my defeat and defeat is a difficult burden to carry, because in the ashes of defeat I am ashamed.

All the loose ends, all the unfinished works that seem to be left hanging in the great defeat of Calvary were brought to completion in the triumph of Christ rising from the ashes of death. In the same way, from the ashes of my defeat, from the shame for sin, Christ arises in me. Christ arises in us and among us so that we are purified and led to the Father, who is our happiness. My defeat is my refusal to give, and the enemy who defeats me is me.

And so, brothers, I tell you that I am sorry for where I have failed and I ask you to join me as I pray for all the goodness that is Christ:
     "Give light to my eyes that I
     may never sleep in death lest
     my enemy say 'I have overcome him.' "

Session III—Communal Penance Service Two

ENTRANCE HYMN AND ENTHRONEMENT OF
THE BIBLE (Stand)

Priest: In the name of the Father, and of the Son, and of the Holy Spirit.
All: Amen.
Priest: Let us pray. (Kneel)
All: Heavenly Father, our hearts are open to you, our wishes are known to you, and you also know our secrets: may the life of your Son be present in our hearts through the Holy Spirit, and may we know and love you more and more every day that we live; we pray through Jesus Christ our Savior, our friend and our brother. Amen.

Psalm 119—(to be recited by the entire community).

> *Ant.: Blessed are those whose way is blameless, who walk in the law of the Lord.*
> *How can a youth remain pure?*
> > *By behaving as your word prescribes.*
>
> *I have sought you with all my heart.*
> > *Do not let me stray from your commandments.*
>
> *I have treasured your promises in my heart,*
> > *since I have no wish to sin against you.*
>
> *How blessed are you, O Lord!*
> > *Teach me your statutes!*
>
> *With my lips I have repeated them,*
> > *all these rulings from your own mouth.*
>
> *In the way of your decrees lies my joy,*
> > *a joy beyond all wealth.*
>
> *I mean to meditate on your precepts*
> > *and to concentrate on your paths.*
>
> *I find my delight in your statutes,*
> > *I do not forget your word.*
>
> *Ant.: Blessed are those whose way is blameless, who walk in the law of the Lord.*

READING.

HOMILY.

COMMUNITY CONFESSION   Anyone who wishes to may publicly confess a fault or failing, ending with: "I ask for pardon." All then say: "Your forgiveness we pray, O Lord."

THE PRECEPTS OF THE LORD FROM THE WORD OF GOD:
(Be seated)

Leader: Happy are the poor in spirit; theirs is the kingdom of heaven.
All: Lord Jesus, make us poor in spirit!
Leader: Happy the gentle: they shall have the earth for their heritage!

All:	Lord Jesus, for the sake of others make us gentle!
Leader:	Happy those who mourn; they shall be comforted.
All:	Lord Jesus, may we always mourn for the harm we have caused others!
Leader:	Happy those who hunger and thirst for what is right: they shall be satisfied.
All:	Lord Jesus, may we always hunger and thirst for what is right!
Leader:	Happy the merciful: They shall have mercy shown them.
All:	Lord Jesus, may we always be merciful!
Leader:	Blessed be the pure in heart: they shall see God.
All:	Lord Jesus, may we see and come to the Father!
Leader:	Happy the peace makers: they shall be called the sons of God.
All:	Lord Jesus, may we too be called peacemakers for the sake of other so that we and all of God's family may be called true sons of the Father!
Leader:	Happy those who are persecuted in the cause of right: theirs is the kingdom of heaven.
All:	Lord Jesus, give us the heart in the face of all difficulties to serve you and our brothers in this life the Father has given us. May we be true and faithful to the last! Amen.

PAUSE FOR EXAMINATION OF CONSCIENCE.

Psalm 51—*Miserere*

Have mercy on me, O God, in your goodness, in your great tenderness wipe away my faults; wash me clean of my guilt, purify me from my sin.

For I am well aware of my faults, I have my sin constantly in mind, having sinned against none other than you, having done what you regard as wrong.

You are just when you pass sentence on me, blameless when you give judgment. You know I was born guilty, a sinner from the moment of conception.

Yet, since you love sincerity of heart, teach me the secrets of wisdom. Purify me with hyssop until I am clean; wash me until I am whiter than snow.

Instill some joy and gladness into me, let the bones you have crushed rejoice again. Hide your face from my sins, wipe out all my guilt.

God, create a clean heart in me, put into me a new and constant spirit, do not banish me from your presence, do not deprive me of your holy spirit.

Be my Savior again, renew my joy, keep my spirit steady and willing; and I shall teach transgressors the way to you, and to you the sinners will return.

Save me from death, God my Savior, and my tongue will acclaim your righteousness; Lord, open my lips, and my mouth will speak out your praise.

Sacrifice gives you no pleasure; were I to offer holocaust, you

*would not have it. My sacrifice is this broken spirit; you will
not scorn this crushed and broken heart.*

*Show your favor graciously to Zion, rebuild the walls of Jerusalem.
Then there will be proper sacrifice to please you—holocaust
and whole oblation—and young bulls to be offered on your
altar.*

Priest: May the peace of Christ remain with you always.
All: Amen.

HYMN.

Session IV—Sacramental Penance Service

I. Benediction Hymn and Enthronement of the Blessed Sacrament

II. Homily

III. Service
    A. "Profession of Faith" Level

        1. Community recitation of Psalm 104 (p. 886 in *Jerusalem Bible*)

        2. Private meditation on sacred Scripture reading

        3. Community recitation of Nicene Creed as response to Yahweh's Word

        4. Penitential song (e.g., "Remember Me")

    B. "Confession of Guilt" Level

        1. Community recitation of Galatians 5:13-24 (p. 327 in *Jerusalem Bible*)

        2. Period of private, personal examination of conscience

        3. Litany of faults—to each accusation please respond, "Lord, we beg your forgiveness." After the lector reads the list of general accusations, please feel free to mention additional community failures or, if you care, a personal admission of guilt.

        4. Community recitation of *Confiteor:*
           I confess to Yahweh; to Blessed Mary, ever a virgin; to St. Michael, the archangel; to St. John the Baptist; to the holy apostles Peter and Paul; to our holy father St. Francis; to all the saints; AND TO YOU, BROTHERS; that I have sinned in thought, word, and deed. This happened through my own fault, my own fault, my own personal fault. Therefore, I entreat Blessed Mary, ever a virgin; St. Michael, the archangel; St. John the Baptist; the holy apostles Peter and Paul; our holy father St. Francis; all the saints; AND YOU, BROTHERS; to pray to Yahweh for me.

Brothers, may Almighty God have mercy on us, forgive us our failures, and bring us to eternal salvation. Amen.

Brothers, may the all-powerful and merciful Lord grant us pardon, absolution, and remission of our offenses. Amen.

    5. Song by select group

C. "Praise, Joy, and Thanksgiving" Level
    1. Community recitation of Psalm 40 (p. 822 in *Jerusalem Bible*)

    2. Turn toward your brother, either beside you or behind you (whomever is more convenient) and recite slowly to each other, in unison with the entire community:
The Lord bless you and keep you. The Lord make his face shine on you and be gracious to you. The Lord lift up his countenance to you and give you peace (making the Sign of the Cross on yourself): In the name of the Father, and of the Son, and of the Holy Spirit. Amen.

IV. Benediction

V. Recessional—"Sing, Sing, Sing"

Session V—Communal Penance Service Three

Feast: Exaltation of the Holy Cross

Vespers

The Way of the Cross—Opening Prayer (Kneel)

Christ, our Brother, we have made these Stations many times before, still we must honestly admit that we seldom recognize you once we leave the church. As we meditate on your sufferings and death, come alive for us a little more this time around. We offer the Way of the Cross in atonement for the sufferings we and our fellowmen continue to heap upon you as you live with us today. Please help us stop crucifying you and grant realization to the statement that "the joys and hopes, the griefs and anxieties of the men of this age, especially those who are poor or in any way afflicted, these are the joys and hopes, the griefs and anxieties of the followers of Christ. Indeed, nothing genuinely human fails to raise an echo in their hearts."

(Opening words of the Constitution on the Church in the Modern World of Vatican II.)

After the 12th Station—Veneration of the Holy Relic—concluding of stations.

Hymn (Penitential; stand)

The Community's Confession (Response to each accusation:
"Your forgiveness we pray, O Lord."

Psalm 49—to be recited by all in unison. (Kneel)

Assemble my faithful before me
who sealed my covenant by sacrifice!
Let the heavens proclaim his righteousness
when God himself is judge.

Listen, my people, I am speaking;
Israel, I am giving evidence against you!
I charge, I indict you to your face,
I, God, your God.

I am not finding fault with your sacrifices,
those holocausts constantly before me;
I do not claim one extra bull from your homes,
nor one extra goat from your pens,

since all the forest animals are already mine,
and the cattle on my mountains in their thousands;
I know all the birds of the air,
nothing moves in the field that does not belong to me.

If I were hungry, I should not tell you,
since the world and all it holds is mine.
Do I eat the flesh of bulls,
or drink goats' blood?

No, let thanksgiving be your sacrifice to God,
fulfill the vows you make to the Most High;
then you can invoke me in your troubles
and I will rescue you, and you shall honour me.

But to the wicked man God says:

What business have you reciting my statutes,
standing there mouthing my covenant,
since you detest my discipline
and thrust my words behind you?

You make friends with a thief as soon as you see one,
you feel at home with adulterers,
your mouth is given freely to evil
and your tongue to inventing lies.

You sit there, slandering your own brother,
you malign your own mother's son.
You do this, and expect me to say nothing?
Do you really think I am like you?

You are leaving God out of account; take care!
Or I will tear you to pieces where no one can rescue you!

Whoever makes thanksgiving his sacrifice honors me;
to the upright man I will show how God can save.

Individual Examination of Conscience and Confession

Psalm 50—to be recited by all in unison. (Common Penance; kneel)

> Have mercy on me, O God, in your goodness,
> in your great tenderness wipe away my faults;
> wash me clean of my guilt,
> purify me from my sin.
> For I am well aware of my faults,
> I have my sin constantly in mind,
> having sinned against none other than you,
> having done what you regard as wrong.
> You are just when you pass sentence on me,
> blameless when you give judgment.
> You know I was born guilty,
> a sinner from the moment of conception.
> Yet, since you love sincerity of heart,
> teach me the secrets of wisdom.
> Purify me with hyssop until I am clean;
> wash me until I am whiter than snow.
> Instill some joy and gladness into me,
> let the bones you have crushed rejoice again.
> Hide your face from my sins,
> wipe out all my guilt.
> God, create a clean heart in me,
> put into me a new and constant spirit,
> do not banish me from your presence,
> do not deprive me of your holy spirit.
> Be my Savior again, renew my joy,
> keep my spirit steady and willing;
> and I shall teach transgressors the way to you,
> and to you the sinners will return.
> Save me from death, God my Savior,
> and my tongue will acclaim your righteousness;
> Lord, open my lips,
> and my mouth will speak out your praise.
> Sacrifice gives you no pleasure,
> were I to offer holocaust, you would not have it.
> My sacrifice is this broken spirit,
> you will not scorn this crushed and broken heart.
> Show your favor graciously to Zion,
> rebuild the walls of Jerusalem.
> Then there will be proper sacrifice to please you
> —holocaust and whole oblation—
> and young bulls to be offered on your altar.

Blessing (by all the Fathers)

Benediction

II. MODEL SCRIPTURE SERVICES

by Maury Smith, O.F.M.

TALKS/EXERCISES

Session I—Christ Our King

HYMN　To Jesus Christ, our sovereign King
Who is the world's salvation,
All praise and homage do we bring
And thanks and adoration.

Christ Jesus, Victor! Christ Jesus, Ruler!
Christ Jesus, Lord and Redeemer.

Enthronement of the Bible.

Prayer:　The Call of the King.
Rt.:　Why are you so frightened, you men of little faith (Matthew 8:26)?
Lf.:　I have come so that you may have life and have it to the full (John 10:10).
Rt.:　If anyone has ears to hear, let him listen to this (Matthew 4:23).
Lf.:　Come to me, all you who labor and are overburdened, and I will give you rest. Shoulder my yoke and learn from me, for I am gentle and humble in heart (Matthew 12:28).
Rt.:　When you stand in prayer, forgive whatever you have against anybody, so that your Father in heaven may forgive your failings too (Mark 11:25).
Lf.:　What I want is mercy, not sacrifice (Amos 5:21). And indeed I did not come to call the virtuous, but sinners (Matthew 9:13, 12:7; Mark 2:17).
Rt.:　You are my friends if you do what I command you. I call you friends because I have made known to you everything I have learned from my Father.
Priest:　I tell you solemnly once again, if two of you on earth agree to ask anything at all, it will be granted to you by my Father in heaven. For when two or three meet in my name, I shall be there with them (Matthew 18:20).
Lf.:　Unless a wheat grain falls on the ground and dies, it remains only a single grain; but if it dies it yields a rich harvest. Anyone who loves his life loses it. Anyone who hates his life in this world will keep it for the eternal life.
Rt.:　If anyone wants to be a follower of mine, let him renounce himself and take up his cross and follow me (Matthew 16:24-25).
Lf.:　For anyone who wants to save his life will lose it; but anyone who loses his life for my sake and for the sake of the Gospel will save it (Matthew 16:26).

Rt.:	Many who are first will be last, and last, first (Matthew 19:30).
Lf.:	Can you drink the cup that I am going to drink (Matthew 20:22)?
Rt.:	Put your sword back, for all who draw the sword will die by the sword (Matthew 26:53).
Lf.:	But I say this to you who are listening—love your enemies, do good to those who hate you, bless those who curse you, pray for those who treat you badly (Luke 6:27).
Rt.:	But I say this to you: love your enemies and pray for those who persecute you (Matthew 6:44).
Lf.:	Do not judge and you will not be judged (Matthew 7:1).
Rt.:	So always treat others as you would like them to treat you (Matthew 7:12).

SCRIPTURE READING Matthew 25:31-46 Feed, clothe, visit the poor, sick and imprisoned; Mark 10:41-45 Leadership with service.

RESPONSE I am the Son of God
I am the true vine
I am the way, the truth and the life
I am the light of the world
I am the good shepherd
I am the bread of life who has come from heaven
I am the gate to everlasting life
I am the resurrection and the life.

Homily: Vatican II Constitution on the Laity

HYMN Thy reign extend, O king benign
to every land and nation
for in thy kingdom, Lord divine,
alone we find salvation.

Christ Jesus, Victor! Christ Jesus, Ruler!
Christ Jesus, Lord and Redeemer.

Gospel Reading: John 13:1-16 Christ washes feet.

Homily: The Christian as one who serves.

Closing Prayer:

Rt.:	Anyone who does the will of my Father in heaven, he is my brother and sister and mother (Matthew 12:50; Mark 3:35).
Lf.:	My mother and my brothers are those who hear the word of God and put it into practice (Luke 8:21).
Rt.:	You must love the Lord your God with all your heart, with all your soul and with all your mind. You must love your neighbor as yourself (Matthew 22:37-40).
Lf.:	Be compassionate as your Father is compassionate. Do not judge and you will not be judged yourselves; do not

condemn and you will not be condemned yourselves; grant pardon and you will be pardoned.

Rt.: Give and there will be gifts for you, a full measure, pressed down, shaken together, and running over, will be poured into your lap, because the amount you measure out is the amount you will be given back (Luke 6:36-38).

Lf.: The greatest among you must be your servant. Anyone who exalts himself will be humbled, and anyone who humbles himself will be exalted (Matthew 23:12).

Rt.: For the Son of Man himself did not come to be served but to serve and to give his life as a ransom for many (Mark 10:45).

Priest: If I then the Lord and Master have washed your feet, you should wash each other's feet. I have given you an example so that you may copy what I have done to you (John 13:14-15).

Rt.: I tell you most solemnly, whoever believes in me will perform the same works as I do myself (John 14:12).

Lf.: If anyone loves me he will keep my word and my Father will love him and we shall come to him and make our home with him (John 14:23).

Blessing with Bible (Please stand).

HYMN To thee and to thy Church, great King
We pledge our heart's oblation,
Until before thy throne we sing
In endless jubilation.

Christ Jesus, Victor! Christ Jesus, Ruler!
Christ Jesus, Lord and Redeemer.

Session II—

The Gospel through Garfunkel
(and 20th century Simon)
and Isaiah
and Matthew
and Tillich
and Boyd
et al.!

Liturgist: By men of strange lips and with an alien tongue,
Congregation: The Lord will speak to his people.
Lit: Lord have mercy upon us.
Cong: Christ have mercy on us.

I

Lit:	The haughtiness of men shall be brought low.
Cong:	The pride of men shall be humbled.
Lit:	The Lord of hosts has a day
Cong:	Against all that is proud and lofty.
Lit:	Men shall enter the caves of the rocks
Cong:	And the holes of the ground.
Lit:	Our idols will be cast forth to the moles and the bats.
Cong:	Men shall enter the caverns of the rocks and the clefts of the cliffs.
Lit:	The Lord of hosts has a day.
Cong:	Those who live by the sword shall perish by the sword.

What was Hiroshima like when the bomb fell? Tell us, Lord, that we, the living, are capable of the same cruelty, the same horror if we turn our backs on you, our brother, and our other brothers. Save us from ourselves: spare us the evils of our hearts: good intentions, unbridled and mad. Turn us from our perversions of love, especially when these are perpetrated in your name. Speak to us about war and about peace, and about the possibilities for both in our very human hearts.

"The Sun Is Burning"

II

Lit:	Having ears to hear we do not hear.
Cong:	Having eyes to see we do not see.
Lit:	How strange we are to each other.
Cong:	How estranged life is from life.
Lit:	Each one of us draws back into himself.
Cong:	Each one of us is self-protected from the cries of the anguished.
Lit:	There is something in the misfortune of our best friends which does not displease us.
Cong:	But we are dishonest enough to deny that this is true.
Lit:	We are almost always ready to abuse everybody and everything for the pleasure of self-elevation,
Cong:	For an occasion for boasting, for a moment of lust.
Lit:	Having ears to hear we do not hear.
Cong:	Having eyes to see we do not see.

I wasn't going to get lonely any more, and so I kept very busy . . . but it's getting dark again, and I'm alone: honestly, Lord, I'm really lonely. Why do I feel sorry for myself? There's no reason why I should be. You're with me, and I know it. I'll be with other people in a little while. I know some of them love me very much in their own way, and I love some of them very much in mine. Give me patience and love so that I can listen when I plug into these other lives. Help me to listen and listen and listen, and love by being quiet and serving, and being there.

"The Sounds of Silence"

III

Lit:	A sparrow falters.
Cong:	Life goes on.
Lit:	A sparrow falters.
Cong:	The unwanted of creation,
Lit:	Yet forever received and affirmed.
Cong:	Even the sparrow finds a home.
Lit:	You are accepted,
Cong:	Accepted by that which is greater than you.
Lit:	Do not ask for the name now.
Cong:	Do not try to do anything now.
Lit:	Do not seek for anything, perform anything, or intend anything.
Cong:	Simply accept the fact that you are accepted,
Lit:	Forever received and affirmed.
Cong:	Even the sparrow finds a home.

I've searched for community in many places. I was often looking in the wrong places, but I don't think my motives were altogether wrong. I was looking futilely and hopelessly there for fellowship, belonging, and acceptance. Now, in this moment, which many people would label "loneliness," or "nothingness," I have found community where and as it is. It seems to me it is your gift. I am here with these others for only a few hours. I will be gone tomorrow. But I won't be searching so desperately any more. I know I must accept community where you offer it to me. I accept it in this moment.

"Sparrow"

IV

Lit:	Send me.
Cong:	But where, Lord? To do what?
Lit:	To bring pardon where there had been injury in a life I casually brush against in my daily life?
Cong:	But I had thought of mediating a teenage gang war in Chicago!
Lit:	To help turn doubt into faith in a person with whom I live intimately in my circle of family or friends?
Cong:	But I thought of helping a tired drunk on skid row!
Lit:	To bring joy into a life, consumed by sadness, which touches the hem of my life at a drinking fountain?
Cong:	But I had thought only of a far-off mission land?
Lit:	Send me. Send me next door, into the next room to speak somehow to a human heart beating alongside mine. Send me to show forth joy in a moment and a place where there is otherwise no joy but only the will to die.

Cong: Send me to reflect your light in the darkness of futility, mere existence, and the horror of casual human cruelty. But give me your light, too, Lord, in my own darkness and need. Amen.

The liturgist acknowledges the use of excerpts from Isaiah, Matthew, the writings of the late Dr. Paul Tillich, and the prayers of Malcolm Boyd from *Are You Running with Me, Jesus?* The three Simon and Garfunkel songs are from their album, "Wednesday Morning, 3 a.m."

Session III—Awake: Praise, Beauty, Awareness

Leader: O God come to our assistance.

All: O Lord make us aware of your presence.
Glory be . . .

PSALM 29   *1 Ant:*   We need to give thanks to our God.

We need to give credit to whom credit is due.
    God is alive, deserving our praises.
There is reason for rejoicing.
    There is a God to worship and love.
His beauty is manifest in the skies and forests.
    His power is represented in the sweep of the ocean.
His majesty is portrayed in the gigantic bodies
    suspended in our universe.
The wind and the rain, lightning and thunder,
    the creatures that inhabit the earth,
the flowers that brighten our lives:
    all this comes from God's hands.
    The glory is not ours, but God's.
Even the achievements of man's mind and hand
    come by way of the wisdom and power of our God.
The contributions of science,
    the fields that ripen for harvest,
the control of our rivers,
    the activities of our cities,
the establishment of our institutions:
    these also reflect God's glory.
Let us rejoice in the God who blesses us.
    Let us give credit to whom credit is due.
Let us seek his grace to serve him,
    by serving others, with the abundance he bestows
        upon us.
Glory be . . .

1 Ant: We need to give thanks to our God.

2 Ant: He makes his presence known.

Wherever I am, wherever I go,

I can sense something of the power of God.
The grandeur of the mountains,
 the vastness of the oceans,
 the breathtaking wonder of interstellar space:
 all this proclaims
 the glory and majesty of God.
Even amid the clutter of our cities,
 built and abused by the hands of men,
 there are reflections of divine splendor.
Heaven's silence or earth's clamor
 may not be very articulate.
 yet God's voice can be heard.
He makes his presence known
 throughout the world.
God has made for man
 a path he is to walk in.
In his will there is order and purpose.
He has proclaimed and demonstrated eternal truth
 through the lips and lives of his children.
There are set before the sons of men
 precepts and principles which direct
 his children in the way of peace and joy.
He has given meaning to life,
 goal and objective to this existence.
Therein is the answer to man's inner need,
 the fulfillment of his deepest longings.
These things are more precious
 and of greater value.
More than anything a man could ever experience
 or even dare to imagine.
This is the course I must follow.
 It is not easy; I make so many mistakes.
I am plagued by my faults and obsessions.
 Forbid, Lord, that these should destroy me.
Set me free from their hold on me.
 Encompass me with your love and grace
 that these things may stand behind and not between
 you and me.
Glory be . . .

2 Ant: He makes his presence known.

3 Ant: You encompass me with love.

O God, in the grace and strength you daily grant,
 your servant finds reason for celebration.
You have truly fulfilled his innermost longings.
 You have encompassed him with security.
He asked for security,
 and you encompassed him with love, also.
He looked to you for life,
 and you gave him eternal life.

He sought for identity,
    and you adopted him as your son.
Whatever is of value and worth in his life
    has come by way of your rich blessings.
His heart is glad in the realization
    of your eternal presence.
He knows that you will never leave,
    nor will you refuse him love.
I raise my voice in praise, O God,
    because no one can separate me from you.
Though circumstances threaten me,
    and my own obsessions entangle me,
    you will never let me go.
Your great power is sufficient to set me free
    from these things that hurt my soul.
If I put my trust in you,
    you will never allow them to destroy me.
I find so many reasons
    for praising you my God.
Glory be . . .

3 Ant: You encompass me with love.

Meditation Song (any selection on beauty)

Leader: The Lord be with you.
All: And also with you.
Leader: Let us pray:
          O God, these are the thoughts that crowd our hearts today. Accept them and respond to them. Enable us to realize anew the security and serenity your presence provides for us. Help us to always be thankful. Help us to always realize and say, "It's a beautiful day, God is here—let's celebrate!" This we ask . . .

Session IV—Communal Penance

Passing of the Holy Scriptures from hand to hand.
    During the passing of the Scriptures, a song shall be sung alternating with the read Word of God.

Preparation of the heart to receive the Word of God.

Priest: Brothers, let us pray with one heart and with one mind to the Holy Spirit!

Community: Almighty God, to whom all hearts are open, all desires known, and from whom no secrets are hidden: Cleanse the thoughts of our hearts by the inspiration of your Holy Spirit, that we may perfectly love you, and with a right heart praise your Holy Name; through Jesus Christ, your Son, our Lord. Amen.

Priest: I ask you in the presence of God, who searches the heart: Do you promise with your whole heart to forgive and love your brothers, as you believe that God forgives and loves you, and to serve him from this time forth in newness of love, to the glory of his Holy Name?

Community: I do so promise!

Priest: Let us kneel, and make this act of penitence to God, imploring his mercy and grace through Jesus Christ our Lord.

Community: O God, our heavenly Father, I confess to you that I have grievously sinned against you and my brothers in many ways; not only by outward transgressions, but also by secret thoughts and desires which I cannot fully understand, but which are all known to you. I do earnestly repent and am heartily sorry for these my offenses, and I beseech you in your great goodness to have mercy on me, and for the sake of your dear Son, Jesus Christ our Lord, to forgive my sins and graciously help my infirmities. Amen!

Our Father. . . .

Priest: O Lord, hear our prayer.

Community: And let our cry come unto you.

Priest: The Lord gives strength to his people.

Community: The Lord blesses his people with peace.

Priest: Let us pray.

Community: O God, you desire that your Church bear witness to you among all nations; grant to this community and to all your faithful people, amid the labors and distresses of this present time, boldness to confess your name; enable us, by your Holy Spirit, to be among our fellowmen as those who serve, turning the hearts of men to you, uplifting the weak, comforting the sorrowing, and speaking peace to the desolate and afflicted; through Jesus Christ, our Lord, who lives and reigns with you and the Holy Spirit, one God, world without end. Amen.

Reading of the Word of God.

The Message.

Discussion.

Handshake of brotherly peace.

The Blessing:
(*Priest*) The Lord bless you and keep you. The Lord make his face shine on you, and be gracious to you. The Lord lift up his countenance upon you, and give you peace: In the name of the Father and of the Son, and of the Holy Spirit. Amen.

Closing Hymn.

Session V—Christian Unity

OPENING HYMN   "Where Charity and Love Prevail"

Priest: Let us pray.

Sovereign Lord, ruler of the universe, look down from heaven upon your Church, upon all your people, and upon your little flock, and save all of us, your unworthy servants, the creatures of your flock, and give us your peace, love, and assistance. Send down upon us the free gift of your Holy Spirit so that with a clean heart we may meet one another with holy love, not deceitfully or hypocritically, nor to control each other's freedom, but blamelessly and purely in the bonds of peace and love. For there is only one body, and one Spirit, and one faith, as we have been called in one hope of our calling so that we might all come to you and to your infinite love in Jesus Christ, our Lord, with whom you are blessed with your all-holy, good, and life-giving Spirit, now and through endless ages.

All: Amen.

Reading: 1 Corinthians 1:10-13.

Short Meditation.

PSALM 24   *The world and all that is in it belong to the Lord;*
     the earth and all who live in it are his.
He built it on the deep waters beneath the earth
     and laid its foundations in the ocean depths.
Who has the right to go up the Lord's hill?
     Who is allowed to enter his holy temple?
He who is pure in act and in thought,
     who does not worship idols, or make false promises.
The Lord will bless him;
     God his Savior will declare him innocent.
Such are the people who come to God,
     who come into the presence of the God of Jacob.
Fling wide the gates, open the ancient doors,
     and the great king will come in!
Who is this great king?
     He is the Lord, strong and mighty, the Lord, victorious in
     battle!
Fling wide the gates, open the ancient doors,
     and the great king will come in!
Who is this great king?
     The Lord of armies, he is the great king!

PSALMS 133, 134   *How wonderful it is, how pleasant,*
     for God's people to live together like brothers!
It is like the precious olive oil running from Aaron's head and
     beard, down to the collar of his robes.
It is like the dew on Mount Hermon,
     falling on the hills of Zion.

That is where the Lord has promised his blessing,
life that never ends.
Come praise the Lord, all his servants,
all who serve in his temple at night.
Raise your hands in prayer in the temple,
and praise the Lord!
May the Lord who made heaven and earth
bless you from Zion.

BENEDICTION HYMN   "O Jesus, We Adore Thee"

CLOSING HYMN   "Faith of Our Fathers"

Session VI—Hope

Entrance Hymn: "A Mighty Fortress Is Our God"

Introduction

PRAYER   Father, we come to you now in silence, yet shouting for joy. We come in silence overawed by the thought of your love for us. You rule supreme over time and space, yet you loved us so much that you gave your only Son to suffer and die for us. To think that you love us like that takes our breath away. We are struck dumb. There is nothing we can say.

And yet, we cannot stay silent when we think of your love for us. You gave us new birth into a living hope when you brought Jesus back from death; so that we could make a new start in life free from the guilt and shame of the past, confident that nothing in death or life can separate us from your love. Father, accept our worship and praise both silent and spoken through Jesus Christ our Lord.

Reading: We look forward with eagerness to the fulfillment of our hope in heaven (2 Corinthians 5:1-10).

Responsorial Hymn: Deiss 5 "Sion Sing," Verses 4-6

Reading Homily Meditation

CLOSING PRAYER   Lord our God, great, eternal, wonderful, utterly to be trusted: you give life to us all, you help those who come to you, you give hope to those who appeal to you. Forgive our sins, secret and open, and rid us of every habit of thought which is foreign to the Gospel. Set our hearts and consciences at peace, so that we may bring our prayers to you confidently and without fear; through Jesus Christ our Lord.

Session VII—Love Poured Out

Priest: We all know that love consists of deeds rather than words, and that the lover shares all that he has and possesses with his beloved. Our daily human experience of life and of love tells us that these things are true. But all our human experience of love is only a shadow and a trace of what Yahweh's love is. Yahweh is love without end. He is love without boundary or limit. He is love without caution, without a breaking-point. Yahweh is love without end. If love means to make a gift of oneself to the beloved, then Yahweh is the greatest lover of all time and beyond time: Yahweh sends us his Spirit to join us to the body of Christ, his son. Standing in the presence of the maker of heaven and earth, we are not called his servants but his friends. And, by way of response Yahweh makes upon us the simple demand of love: "My son, give me your heart" (Proverbs 26:26).

ALL STAND

All: The love of Yahweh has been poured out in our hearts by the Holy Spirit, whom we have received.

Priest: I am sure that neither death, nor life, nor angels, nor principalities, nor things present, nor things to come, nor any other creature will be able to separate us from the love of Yahweh which is in Christ Jesus our Lord.

All: The love of Yahweh has been poured out in our hearts by the Holy Spirit, whom we have received.

ALL SIT

Priest: Let us listen to the inspired words of the psalmist, who gives us a hymn of praise for the wonders of creation, the gift of Yahweh's love for us.

Reader: Psalm 103.

ALL KNEEL

Priest: Let us pray, giving thanks to Yahweh for the love he has shown us in the wonders of creation.
(Pause for personal prayer)
All things have been created through Christ and are to be restored through Christ to the Father.

All: Father, accept the offering we make with Christ our brother.

Priest: Christ has made all earth holy.

All: Father, accept the offering, etc.

Priest: Christ has sanctified the seasons of nature's year.

All: Father, accept the offering, etc.

Priest: Christ has sanctified the hours of both day and night.

All: Father, accept the offering, etc.

Priest: Christ has sanctified all that the earth yields.

All: Father, accept the offering, etc.

Priest: Christ has sanctified everything that lives on the earth, in the sea and in the skies.

All: Father, accept the offering, etc.

Priest: Christ has sanctified man and all the works of man.

All: Father, accept the offering, etc.

Priest: Christ has sanctified our deepest thoughts, every plan that we make, every hope that we possess, our every act of love.

All: Glory be to the Father, etc.

ALL SIT *Priest:* Let us listen now to the first letter of St. John, whose inspired words teach us that our Christian life is a life of love.

Reader: 1 John 4:7-16.

All: God is love and he who abides in love abides in God and God in him (sing).

ALL KNEEL *Priest:* Let us pray, begging God for the grace to offer our whole selves in a sacrifice of love to him.
(Pause for personal prayer)
He who has my commandments and keeps them, he it is who loves me.

All: Take, O Lord, and receive all my liberty, my memory, my understanding and my entire will.

Priest: He who loves me will be loved by my Father, and I will love him and manifest myself to him.

All: Take, O Lord, and receive all that I have and possess.

Priest: If anyone love me, he will keep my word, and my Father will love him, and we will come to him and make our abode with him.

All: Lord, you have given me everything. I return it all to you.

Priest: As the Father has loved me, I also have loved you. Abide in my love.

All: Lord, dispose of everything that I have according to your holy will.

Priest: Greater love than this no one has, that one lay down his life for his friends.

All: Lord Jesus, only give us your love and your grace; this is sufficient for us.

Priest: Let us pray, asking the Lord for the grace of a whole-hearted generosity in the love that we return to him.
(Pause for personal prayer)
Lord, teach us to be generous. Teach us to serve you as you deserve; to give and not to count the cost; to fight and not to heed the wounds; to toil and not to seek for rest; to labor and not to ask for any reward, save that of knowing that we do your will; through Christ our Lord.

All: Amen. The love of Yahweh has been poured out in our hearts by the Holy Spirit, whom we have received.

Priest: I am sure that neither death, nor life, nor angels, nor principalities, nor things present, nor things to come, nor any other creature will be able to separate us from the love of Yahweh which is in Christ Jesus our Lord.

All: The love of Yahweh has been poured out in our hearts by the Holy Spirit, whom we have received.

| | *All:* | What the world needs now is love sweet love (sing). |

Session VIII—God's Presence

Leader: (Introduction by leader)

ALL STAND *All:* My heart and my flesh cry out for the living God.
Leader: I stand at the door and knock; if anyone hears my voice and opens the door, I will come into his house and eat with him, and he will eat with me.
All: My heart and my flesh cry out for the living God.

ALL SIT *Leader:* (Introduction to reading)

Reader: (First reading)

At the conclusion of the reading, *all kneel.*

Leader: Nothing is too wonderful for the Lord! Let us pray, giving thanks for the loving care which the Lord shows in all the events of our lives.
(Pause for personal prayer)
If anyone hears my voice and opens the door, I will come into his house and eat with him and he will eat with me.
All: O God, you are my God whom I seek.
Leader: Lord, come and dwell in the midst of our daily lives.
All: O God, you are my God whom I seek.
Leader: Lord, sanctify us in our eucharistic sacrifice.
All: O God, you are my God whom I seek.
Leader: Lord, come to consecrate the hours of our daily work.
All: O God, you are my God whom I seek.
Leader: Lord, come and dwell in the midst of our community life.
All: O God, you are my God whom I seek.
Leader: Lord, come and sit with us at our meals.
All: O God, you are my God whom I seek.
Leader: Lord, come and share the joy of our recreation.
All: O God, you are my God whom I seek.
Leader: Lord, come to watch over the hours of our rest.
All: O God, you are my God whom I seek.
Leader: Lord, come to enlighten the decisions we make.
All: O God, you are my God whom I seek.
Leader: Lord, come to encourage us in our resolutions.
All: O God, you are my God whom I seek.
Leader: Lord, come to struggle with us against evil.
All: O God, you are my God whom I seek.
Leader: Lord, come and enlarge our hearts so that no one escapes our love.
All: O God, you are my God whom I seek.
Leader: O Lord, come and live within us the members of your body.
All: O God, you are my God whom I seek.

ALL SIT

Leader: (Introduction to reading)

Reader: (Second reading)

At the conclusion of the reading, *all kneel.*

Leader: Let us pray asking the Lord for the grace that all men may share in his Kingdom.
(Pause for personal prayer)
Come, eat of my food and drink of the wine I have mixed.

All: Give all men this day their daily bread.

Leader: Blessed is he who shall feast in the kingdom of God.

All: Give all men this day their daily bread.

Leader: The kingdom of heaven is like a king who gave a wedding feast for his Son.

All: Give all men this day their daily bread.

Leader: I appoint to you a kingdom, even as my Father has appointed me, that you may eat and drink at my table in my kingdom.

All: Give all men this day their daily bread.

Leader: I tell you that many will come from the East and from the West and will feast with Abraham and Isaac and Jacob in the kingdom of heaven.

All: Give all men this day their daily bread.

Leader: Jesus took the five loaves and the two fishes and, looking up to heaven, blessed and broke the loaves, and gave them to the disciples to set before the people.

All: Give all men this day their daily bread.

Leader: Take and eat, this is my body.

All: Give all men this day their daily bread.

Leader: All of you drink of this, for this is the blood of the new covenant, which is being shed for many for the forgiveness of sins.

All: Give all men this day their daily bread.

Leader: I tell you I will never again drink this wine until the day I drink the new wine with you in my Father's kingdom.

All: Give all men this day their daily bread.

ALL STAND

Leader: (Introduction to reading)

Reader: (Third reading)

At the conclusion of the reading, *all sit.*

Homily

After the homily, *all kneel.*

Leader: Let us pray, begging the Lord that he will make his presence known to us.
(Pause for personal prayer)
When we lose sight of the power you hold as Lord and Master of history—

All: Stay with us then, O Lord.

Leader: When we fail to recognize your presence in the events of
our daily lives—
All: Stay with us then, O Lord.
Leader: When we do not remember that it is necessary for us to
suffer and die with you so as to share your glory—
All: Stay with us then, O Lord.
Leader: When we make our minds dull and foolish so that we do
not understand the Word that you speak to us—
All: Stay with us then, O Lord.
Leader: When we are inclined not to face the real situations that
arise in our lives, but prefer to turn from them and from
seeking your will in them—
All: Stay with us then, O Lord.
Leader: When our feelings tell us that the trials you send us are a
sign that you have abandoned us—
All: Stay with us then, O Lord.
Leader: When our impulse to show our love for others degen-
erates into a selfish attempt to satisfy our own needs—
All: Stay with us then, O Lord.
Leader: When the day of our life on earth draws toward evening
and the hand of death tightens its grip on us—
All: Stay with us then, O Lord.
Leader: Let us pray that the Lord will open our hearts to receive
the gift of himself.
(Pause for personal prayer)
O Lord our God in times gone by you visited our Father
Abraham and made yourself known to your people;
today you are present with us as we make our pilgrimage
through this life. Grant we beg you that our eyes may be
opened to recognize you and our hearts set on fire by
your own Spirit of love, now and forever.
All: Amen! My heart and my flesh cry out for the living God.
Leader: I stand at the door and knock; if anyone hears my voice
and opens the door, I will come into his house and eat
with him and he will eat with me.
All: My heart and my flesh cry out for the living God.

Session IX—Evening Service Concerning "Time"

Entrance Hymn.

Leader: "Be most careful about how you conduct yourselves: like
sensible men, not like simpletons. Use the present opportunity to the full. So do not be fools, but try to understand what the will of the Lord is" (Ephesians 5:15-17).

Lord, you have been our refuge age after age.
Before the mountains were born,
before the earth or the world came to birth,
you were God from all Eternity and forever.

You can turn man back into dust
by saying, "Back to what you were, you sons of men!"
To you, a thousand years are a single day,
a yesterday now over, an hour of the night.

You brush men away like waking dreams.
They are like grass,
sprouting and flowering in the morning,
withered and dry before dusk.

Our days dwindle under your gaze,
our lives are over in a breath;
our lives last for seventy years,
eighty with good health.

But they all add up to anxiety and trouble,
over in a moment and then we are gone.
Teach us to count how few days we have
and so gain wisdom of heart.

Let us wake in the morning filled with your love
and sing and be happy all our days.
Let your servants see what you can do for them;
let your children see your glory.

Glory be, etc.

Bless Yahweh, my soul,
bless his holy name, all that is in me.
Bless Yahweh, my soul,
and remember all his kindnesses
in forgiving all your offenses,
in curing all your diseases,
in redeeming your life from the pit,
in crowning you with love and tenderness,
in filling your years with prosperity,
in renewing your youth like an eagle's.

Yahweh, who does what is right
is always on the side of the oppressed;
he never treats us, never punishes us,
as our guilt and our sins deserve.

As tenderly as a father treats his children,
so Yahweh treats those who fear him;
he knows what we are made of;
he remembers we are dust.

Man lasts no longer than grass,
no longer than a wild flower he lives;
one gust of wind, and he is gone,
never to be seen there again.

Yet Yahweh's love for those who fear him
lasts from all eternity and forever.

*Bless Yahweh, all his creatures
in every part of his creation.*

Glory be, etc.

Reading.

Pause for Reflection.

All: All of us complain that we haven't enough time. But we look at our lives from too human a point of view. There is always enough time to do what God wants us to do, but we must put ourselves completely into each moment that he offers us.

Benediction.

III. MODEL HOMILIES

by Bernard Head, Raymond Bosler, Martin Peter

TALKS/EXERCISES

Session I—Change

OUTLINE

I. If the apostles were to return to earth today, they would find quite a different Church from the one they knew.
   A. Size, complexity, and belief
   B. Reactions might be mixed
II. Change is a fact of life which we all must face.
   A. Possibilities: smother, ignore, direct
   B. Need for Christian to direct change
   C. How this is done: desire, patience, trust
III. God asks progressive improvement of us.

HOMILY

If the apostles were to come back to earth today, it is quite possible that they would not recognize their Church. The Roman Catholic Church of the 1970s is quite different, at least in appearance, from the Christian community of the first century.

Today, there are more than 46 million Catholics in the United States alone as compared with the handful of Christians in apostolic times. The Church is also much more complex now than it was then. In earlier days, the business of the Church was transacted rather informally in gatherings of a few Church leaders, such as at the council of Jerusalem. Now it requires innumerable offices, bureaus, and huge assemblies of bishops to get the Church's work done. There is also a difference in belief today, not in *what* we believe but in the *greater insights* we have into the data of our faith. The apostles accepted the fact of the presence of Jesus in the Eucharist as we do. But today, we are asking *how* Jesus is present.

I don't know how the apostles would react to these changes, but if they are typical of mankind generally, one would probably find some of them rejoicing in change and others opposing it.

We are all aware, however, that whether anyone likes it or not, changes do occur. They always have, and they always will. If a thing does not change and grow, either it never had life to start with, or it is dead.

The same thing is true of each individual person. Everyone has the seeds of change in him or her, and whether we notice it or not, we are all always changing. If you have ever been to a family reunion or a gathering of your old graduating class and met people you had not seen perhaps for years, you noticed that they were not as you remembered them. They had changed in some way or other.

If it is true that we are all always changing, it is clear that we have to face this fact and come to terms with change in ourselves. It seems that, in this matter, there are three possibilities open to us. First, we can attempt to smother the seeds of change in us. We can try to remain the same as we always were, feeling that we are satisfied with ourselves as we are. This may seem possible, but in reality it cannot be done. All we need to do to be convinced of this is to look at a picture of ourselves which was taken several years ago.

Second, we can let these seeds of change grow wild, and many people do this. They simply accept changes in themselves without thought or else consider it impossible to do anything about these changes. You often hear people say: "Well, that's just the way I am."

Third, we can direct the growth of these seeds of change. We can try to become what we want to become or what we know we should become. This involves setting goals for ourselves and choosing specific means to reach these goals. Granted that we are going to change, we decide how we want to change and direct our efforts to bringing this about.

It seems to me that the only alternative appropriate for the Christian is the third. This is a constant theme in Paul's letters, especially in 1 and 2 Corinthians where he tells us that a person changes just by becoming a Christian. "Therefore, if anyone is in Christ, he is a new creation." The Christian has entered a new existence, has set his life off on a new course. But, Paul says, change doesn't end here. This new life, signed by baptism, is just the beginning of a continuous change.

St. John, perhaps more than anyone besides Jesus himself, tells us what direction this change should take. He says that we are to grow in love; we are to change into the kind of selfless, generous lover that Jesus was. This is what it means to live in Christ.

If this is so, if we are expected to change progressively for the better as we go through life, how are we to do it? First, I think we must want to change. We must be convinced that it is worthwhile to try and improve ourselves as Christians, to grow in love of God and one another. We must also renew this conviction often or we will find that we are standing still. The goals which we set today are easily choked by the experiences and distractions of tomorrow. I believe it is here that we find our liturgical worship to be very important. In the Eucharist, we publicly commit ourselves to the living of a fully Christian life. We bring to Mass a desire to live in Christ—in love. The Mass is not a Communion machine, not a feat of magic which mysteriously produces Christ on the altar. It is an intensely human experience in which God's people, as a family, renew their commitment to God through, with, and in the Christ who is present to them in the eucharistic celebration.

Second, once we have made up our minds to change for the better, we must be patient. We must realize that we are weak human beings and far from perfect. Improvement is a gradual thing. If we are patient with learning a job, a skill, or a lesson in school, why can we not be patient in the development of our Christian lives?

Third, we must have a great deal of trust in the goodness of God. He will strengthen our weakness and forgive our failures. We must be convinced of that.

"We are being changed into Christ's likeness from one degree of glory to another," says Paul. Progressive improvement, a gradual change for the better, is what God asks of us.

Session II—God

OUTLINE

I. Most Americans believe in God.
II. Kinds of God they believe in: gift-giver, calculator, private eye
III. More satisfactory notion of God involves intimacy
IV. Need to respond to God's desire for intimacy
V. Means: prayer and Scripture

HOMILY

There is a great deal of talk today about our world being materialistic, secularistic, and godless. There is no denying that we have perhaps more than our share of crime and contention, heartless competition and selfishness on our planet.

In view of this, it came as somewhat of a surprise a year or so ago to hear a large polling organization report that most Americans believe in God. In spite of the public image of American morality, in spite of the much publicized difficulties with the institutional Church, in spite of apparent apathy on the part of many toward active participation in religious matters, most people in our country do believe in God.

This was indeed an interesting conclusion. But an even more interesting piece of data would have been an answer to the question as to the kind of God in which they believe. I would suggest that the American people believe in several different kinds of Gods.

Some believe in a gift-giver God. He is able to provide for us everything that we want and need. If we only pray for these things, he will send them to us. These people—the worshipers of the gift-giver God—only turn to him when they are in need and are quite disappointed when the gift-giver doesn't come through.

Some believe in a private-eye God. He is always following them around, looking over their shoulders, and waiting for them to do something wrong so that he can punish them.

Some believe in a calculator God. He is sitting in heaven, totaling up good points for our virtuous acts and bad points for our failings. He will reveal the score to us on judgment day when we will be either pleasantly surprised or eternally disappointed.

These are very different images of God, but they all have one thing in common. They all lack intimacy. One can't get close to any of them. The gift-giver is noticed only when we need him. The private-eye frightens us. And the calculator is impersonal. For this reason, they are all very unsatisfactory notions of God.

Perhaps if we want a more accurate and satisfying idea of

God, we would do well to go to his own Word. We have such an idea in John's Gospel. John doesn't speak of God in any of the terms which we have spoken of so far. When John speaks of God, he calls him Father. In fact, in the course of all of John's writings, he uses the name Father for God one hundred and seven times. He might be trying to tell us something.

I think that what John is trying to tell us is this: God does not want to be distant from us. He wants an intimate relationship with all of us—as intimate as that of father and child. And God has certainly done his part to bring this about. He has told us a lot about himself in Scripture, and he has never referred to himself as an occasional gift-giver, private-eye, or calculator. Furthermore, he has left us his sacramental presence in the Eucharist. And finally, he has sent his Spirit to guide and guard us in the Church.

But intimacy is a two-way street. One person cannot have an intimate relationship with another unless the other responds. A father or mother cannot be intimate with his or her child unless the child is willing to have this kind of relationship. A lover cannot enjoy any kind of intimacy with the beloved unless the beloved reciprocates. And so, no matter how much God wants loving intimacy with us, he cannot and will not force it. We have to respond.

If we want to believe in the real God and not in some caricature of God, we need to think about responding to our Father's offer of intimacy. To do this, we need to pray often, alone and with others, in church and outside of church, in a structured way and in a free-wheeling, informal way.

We need to get to know God better by picking up the Scripture, reading it, and thinking about it.

We need to feel that God *is* Father, that Jesus *is* brother—not just to admit it but to feel it. This can make a great deal of difference in our outlook, our attitudes, and our lives.

We Catholics have a tradition of being a praying people, whether that involved the mystical prayer of the saints, the public prayer of the Mass, or the simple practice of the Rosary and other devotions.

We ought to keep that tradition of prayer alive for our own sakes and in whatever form we find agreeable and helpful. This will aid us immensely in coming to a true notion of what God really is.

The Sacrament of Penance

OUTLINE

I. People are wondering about their changing attitudes toward confession.
II. There are reasons for this change.
   A. A different attitude toward sin
   B. A different attitude toward the sacrament of penance
III. The purpose of the sacrament of penance is to signify repentance and reconciliation.

IV. We have a need to experience this sacrament even with the changes in attitude we have undergone.

HOMILY

I don't know how many times in the past year different people I have been talking with have brought up a certain topic for conversation. It wasn't that I led them into it. Rather, it seemed to be a purely spontaneous thing. This has occurred at different times, in different states, and with many different kinds of people.

The topic which they brought up was confession. They would usually begin by saying: "A funny thing has happened to me. I used to go to confession every week or every month. Now it has been a year or two years since I have been, and it doesn't seem to bother me." They are puzzled by this change in attitude, and they can't really explain it.

It isn't that they made a conscious decision not to go to confession or that they made a study of the history and theology of the sacrament of penance and reasoned this change out for themselves. It simply happened, and they began to notice it.

I think there is a reason for this change, and I believe it has to do with two attitudes—an attitude toward sin and an attitude toward the sacrament of penance itself.

Many people tend to look upon sin as something which they did, an action which they performed. The general pattern of their lives or their intentions had little to do with sin. If I performed this action, I committed a sin—missed Mass, got angry, argued, etc. They felt that many things which they did must have been sins. The sacrament of penance was seen as a kind of automatic process. The words of absolution automatically washed away the sins.

Many of these same people became uncomfortable with these ideas. They felt that their lives weren't really that bad. They became weary of a mechanical recitation of sins and uneasy about routine absolution. After a while, the sacrament of penance really didn't seem to do anything for them.

I feel that it is a good thing that this has happened, because it has caused many of us to take a second look at the sacrament of penance and to deepen our awareness of what it really is and what it is really for.

We have become aware once again that it essentially involves two things. First of all, it involves *repentance*. To repent means to decide to change for the better, to look at the pattern of my life over a period of time and see where I am falling short of what I should be as a person and as a Christian. This assumes that I know what kind of life I should aspire to as a person and as a Christian. If I know what the demands of Christianity are, I find that I am not perfect. I have fallen short of these demands. Then, I decide to do something about this—to improve myself—to reach higher—to change for the better.

Repentance is an inward and deeply personal experience, not just gathering a list of actions. And no one can repent for me. This is one thing that I must do for myself.

The sacrament of penance also involves *reconciliation.* I realize that my failings affect other people. As a Christian, I am part of a community of love—a Church. My failings or sins turn me in on myself and away from others. When I repent, I want to strengthen and increase my loving relationship with the community of believers which my selfishness has harmed.

The sacrament of penance is an outward sign of these two things. The outward sign of my repentance or my change of heart is confession, admitting my intentions to the community or its representative. The outward sign of reconciliation is absolution. This means that God and the community have accepted my word, my efforts to repent.

So the sacrament of penance is not automatic. My personal decision is essential. Nor is it simply a private matter. The community is somehow involved.

If we are going to live lives that are worthwhile to ourselves and others, this process of repentance and reconciliation should be an important part of our experience. How often we approach the sacrament of penance depends, to a great extent, on our readiness and our need. But we all, from time to time, need to come to personal terms with the direction of our lives and to put our efforts to change for the better into the context of the Church.

Session IV—Prayer

OUTLINE

I. If we expect Jesus to have prayed, we, as followers of Jesus, can be expected to pray as well.
II. There are different notions of what successful prayer is.
   A. Practical criteria
   B. Better view
III. Conclusions
   A. God's opinion of us depends on what we are willing to try.
   B. The Lord's Prayer is our model of truly successful prayer.

HOMILY

It is not particularly surprising to read in the Gospel that Jesus went off to pray. As the holy man par excellence, as the Son of God, Jesus was expected to pray. If he didn't pray, we would wonder about him.

As followers of Jesus, we are expected to pray, too, and I am sure that all of us do pray from time to time, more or less successfully. We come to Mass to pray. We make a retreat to pray.

But what is "successful prayer"? Prayer is something we all do, but how do we know if we are doing it the right way or if our prayer is having the effect it should?

I suppose some people would judge the success of their prayer in different ways. The would consider their prayer worthwhile if they received what they prayed for, or if it made them feel good, or if they were able to stick with it over the years, or if they spent enough time at it.

These criteria come easily to mind and are based on a very

practical approach to prayer. But I do not believe that they really get at the heart of what successful prayer is.

I would like to suggest to you in the form of a little quiz some of the elements which I feel add up to successful prayer. You can supply simple yes or no answers for yourselves.

Is my prayer *primary*? Does it spring from a real sense of need, or is it simply a dull chore performed from a sense of duty or fear?

Is my prayer *fresh*? Does it contain some element of wonder in the presence of God? Does it take me out of my small circle of commonplace experience and put me in touch with someone much greater than I? Or is my prayer simply an extension of the often trivial, forced, and artificial communication which I so often experience?

Is my prayer *dynamic*? Does the fact that I pray make a difference in my attitudes and behavior? Is there some carry-over from my prayer that makes me a little more understanding, more loving and a more lovable person?

Is my prayer *growing*? Does my prayer lead me to deeper spiritual insights? As a result of prayer and over a period of time, do I find myself looking at people and things more from God's point of view, that is, not just as objects but also as creatures which have come from God and are destined somehow to return to him?

Is my prayer *God-centered*? In prayer, do I try to bring my will, my hopes, my attitudes into line with those of God? Or is the purpose of my prayer simply to get things for myself or to change God's mind so that he will do what I want?

If we can answer all of these questions with a "yes," if we can say that our prayer is primary, fresh, dynamic, growing, and God-centered, then, I feel, we have achieved real success in prayer.

However, if you are like me, you probably cannot always answer yes to all of these questions about prayer. In fact, you probably cannot even remember what all of the questions are! So I would suggest two things to you:

First of all, God's opinion of us depends not so much on what we achieve as on what we try. If we try to make our prayer as primary, fresh, dynamic, growing, and God-centered as we can, then he will consider it successful even if we do not reach the perfect ideal.

Second, if our notion of what successful prayer ought to be becomes hazy and unclear, I suggest we take a good look at the Lord's Prayer. This is the model Jesus gave us of good prayer, and we can learn much about prayer from it.

During Mass, when we recite the Lord's Prayer together, we have a good opportunity to assimilate the spirit of Jesus' own prayer and to begin to carry this spirit over into our own efforts to pray.

Session V—A Challenge to the Apostolic Layman

OUTLINE   The American Picture
                1. The Race Question

HOMILY

We Americans are an impatient people. We are proud of the fact. We want results, and we want them right now.

We are impatient about almost everything under the sun—*except one thing.*

And about this one thing we are extremely virtuous. We are not only most patient, we are most prudent about it.

The race problem, we say, will not be solved in our lifetime and more than likely, not in many lifetimes. It will be a gradual process, we say, requiring much education of both Negroes and whites. Those who are pushing us into precipitous action, we say, are really setting the cause back many years. We must be prudent; we must be patient.

This is not the way Americans ordinarily approach a problem. This is untypical of America.

And when you come right down to it, everything about the race problem is untypical; it doesn't fit into the American picture.

And that is why we ought to get rid of it. Right away. It is time to approach the race problem in the typical American manner—with impatience, with a determination to get results, immediate results.

Our whole future as a nation may be determined by what we do about the race problem in the next few years. I propose for your consideration that the race problem is the core of all our problems today. What we do about it is the ultimate test of our commitment to democracy; it is the ultimate test of our understanding of Christianity; and it may be the deciding factor in whether God permits the white race to destroy itself in a nuclear holocaust.

Whether we like it or not, other people judge the sincerity of our commitment to democracy by the way we treat the Negroes and other non-white minorities in our midst.

Let a Negro girl be turned away from the University of Georgia, and within six hours a cab driver and his fare in Pakistan will be discussing the failure of democracy in the United States.

Let an African diplomat be refused service in a Maryland restaurant, and within a day a wave of anti-Americanism sweeps a continent where the United States has been supporting the rise of new nations.

No matter how generous we are with the money, food and medicines we send to Asiatic nations, the natives there can easily be stirred up against us by any amateur propagandist who points out how the United States immigration laws imply that Orientals are undesirable.

We Americans, understandably, are hurt by the anti-Americanism that is growing everywhere in the world today—the ingratitude of the nations we have helped, the injustice of overlooking our very considerable virtues and magnifying one fault out of all proportion. It isn't fair.

But there is another way of looking at this.

The neutralist nations, like India, for instance, who were quick to criticize us for aggression in Cuba, though they were significantly silent while the Russians enslaved the Hungarians, may be paying us a compliment by their anti-Americanism.

Anti-Americanism is much like a certain brand of anti-clericalism. The rest of the world expects more of us because we have dedicated ourselves to the works of perfection among nations: to promoting freedom, the brotherhood and equality of man, the right of self-rule. When we fail to live up to these ideals, resentment rises against us as it does against clergymen who fail to practice what they preach.

We are still the great hope of those everywhere who love freedom.

We are the nation of destiny they look to for leadership against all forms of servitude. Since the vast majority of them are colored—yellow, black, and brown—they want to know whether true brotherhood and equality are possible for them on our terms.

There is a social gospel in the democracy we Americans have embraced. It is written large and clear in our Constitution and its amendments. But we have been slow to realize all its implications. There is a vision of brotherhood and equality in it. Outsiders have seen it better than we.

They challenge us now. Are you willing to practice what you preach to us in your Constitution? Will you allow a Negro to buy a home where he can meet the price, eat where he pleases, enjoy recreation where he chooses? Will you judge him for what he is and not by the color of his skin when he applies for a job or offers a hand of friendship? Do you mean what you say, you Americans, or must we, disillusioned, turn to Communist comrades who offer a new plan for brotherhood?

We can't wait a generation to answer those demands. Time has run out on us.

As Christians, we ought to be doubly impatient and eager for an immediate solution to the race problem. With St. Paul we must be saying "the love of Christ impels us" (2 Corinthians 5:14). And what it impels us to do is plain as plain can be in the Gospels. St. John records Jesus as saying: "A new commandment I give you . . . that you love one another as I have loved you" (John 13:34; 15:12).

This was putting new dimensions into the old law, which required one to love his neighbor as he loved himself. Christ will be satisfied with nothing less than a love like his own—a love that requires sacrifice of self for one's neighbor.

And the Gospels spell out relentlessly where this leads.

Our neighbor is not only those of our own race, those of like interests who are attractive to us, but every man redeemed by Jesus Christ. The master's description of how we shall be judged on the way we love or fail to love him in our neighbor is shockingly clear in its detail:

"Then he will say to those on his left hand, 'Depart from me, accursed ones, into the everlasting fire which was prepared for the devil and his angels. For I was hungry, and you did not give me to eat; I was thirsty and you gave me no drink; I was a stranger and you did not take me in; naked, and you did not clothe me; sick and in prison, and you did not visit me!' Then they also will answer and say, 'Lord, when did we see thee hungry, or thirsty, or a stranger, or naked, or sick, or in prison, and did not minister to thee?' Then he will answer them saying: 'Amen I say to you, as long as you did not do it for one of these least ones, you did not do it for me' " (Matthew 25:41-45).

The Negroes are far from being the least of Christ's brethren, but the lesson is clear—as we love or reject Jesus Christ himself. If we refuse to live in the same block with a Negro family, we refuse to live with Jesus Christ. If we turn down a Negro applying for a job merely because he is a Negro, we are turning down Jesus Christ.

"A new commandment I give you, that you love one another as I have loved you."

That requires at the very least that we love the Negro enough to be hurt a bit financially for him; enough to put up with criticism and accept embarrassment for him.

Is this asking too much? Is it possible to keep Christ's new commandment? By ourselves it is impossible. But no Christian is by himself. He is with Christ or he is not a Christian.

"All you who have been baptized into Christ, have put on Christ," says St. Paul (Galatians 3:27). And with Paul every Christian should live so as to be able to say: *"It is now no longer I that live, but Christ lives in me"* (Galatians 2:20). Christ wants to love others in and through us. If we let Christ live in us, we shall be able to observe his new commandment.

Does Christ live in me? Does he love others in me? There is no better test today for an American than to ask himself: What am I doing *for* the Negro? What am I doing *to* the Negro? Do I care?

The race question is the ultimate test of our understanding of Christianity.

And the race question may very well be the last test God is willing to give the white race. At this decisive moment in history the white man, and only the white man, has within his hands the power to destroy himself utterly. One mistake—one vodka too many in the Kremlin or an order misunderstood by our own air command—and Russia and the United States might begin the nuclear holocaust that would destroy North America and Europe.

One thinks at this hour of Abraham Lincoln's reflections on the meaning of the Civil War:

"Insomuch as we know that by his Divine law nations, like individuals, are subjected to punishments and chastisements in this world, may we not justly fear that the awful calamity of civil war which now desolates the land may be but a punishment inflicted upon us for our presumptuous sins, to the needful end of our national reformation as a whole people? We have been the recipients of the choicest bounties of heaven: we have been preserved these many years in peace and prosperity; we have grown in numbers, wealth and power as no nation has ever grown. But have we forgotten God?"

If we had grown in numbers, wealth and power as no nation had ever grown before the Civil War, what must we say of ourselves now?

Through the years we have grown richer and richer while three-fourths of the people of the world have been growing relatively poorer. Not through malice, but through negligence and ignorance, we have failed to fulfill our obligations to these suffering brothers of ours—when we have not actually exploited them.

Should we not look upon Communism itself as a punishment for our sins? For our rugged individualism, for our forgetfulness of the brotherhood of man, for our failure to recognize the unity of the human race, for our ignorance of the social obligations of our religion, God seems to have fashioned a punishment to fit the crime. And like all divine punishments, it seems designed to reform us.

Into the vacuum created by our refusal to live the full Christian life, God permits the enemy to rush in with an imitation of the truth, a travesty of the mystical body. The attraction of Communism is its imitation of God's plan. It appeals to man's desire for brotherhood; it offers a plan for uniting the human race; it asks sacrifices from the individual for the common good of the whole human race. It is revolutionary, as Christianity is designed to be revolutionary. It has set a fire ablaze in the world that can only be stopped by the rekindled fire of Christianity.

"To throw a firebrand upon the earth—that is my mission," said the master, Jesus Christ, *"and, oh, how I wish it were already in a blaze"* (Luke 12:49).

What a pity that he must say it again today.

And while the enemy's fire blazes, what are we doing? We Catholics in the United States are arguing bitterly among ourselves over whether the principal Communist threat is from subversion within or from outside attack. And some of us join anti-Communist organizations that teach us how to go around like beagle hounds with our noses to the ground and our tails swishing patriotically in the air, vainly trying to scare out Communists from government offices, Protestant pulpits and even Catholic editorial offices. Why should a Catholic join any anti-Communist organization? He already belongs to God's own anti-Communist organization.

Our future is totally in God's hands. We are helpless now to avoid nuclear suicide. Only God can save us. And he will save us, if we are worth saving.

The way to overcome Communism is to learn the lesson God is teaching us by permitting Communism. We are being punished for our failure to live the revolutionary social teachings of the Gospel; we are being punished for our failure to recognize the brotherhood of man and the unity of the human race.

Our only successful defense against Communism, therefore, will be to put into practice the lesson God is teaching us. And is that lesson not evident by now? Communism exists: 1. because Christians have not recognized the social implications of the Gospel; 2. because Christians have been nationalistic instead of internationally minded; 3. because the wealthy Christian states have not shared their riches and know-how with less fortunate nations; 4. because the wealthy landowners in so-called Catholic countries have refused to recognize the obligation in social justice to share their wealth with the poor living all around them; 5. because those who bear the name of Christ have failed to see Christ in the Negro, the Chinese, the Mexican. Those are some of the reasons why there is Communism in the world today.

God's punishment is already having some effect. We Americans are awakening to the plight of the have-not nations. We have been generous in recent years. Now at last we are ready to do something for South America. We must confess that our motives are showing and that they are not always as clean as they ought to be, but the Communists are forcing us to accept at last our social obligations to our fellowmen in all parts of the world.

We have only begun. We have not yet shown the change of heart that God expects of us. The race problem gives us our Christian conviction. It gives us what we are all looking for: the chance to strike our blow against Communism.

We are all frustrated today because we feel so helpless before the menace of Communism. So some of us join extremist anti-Communist organizations and blow off steam by slugging away at the reputations of fellow Americans who disagree with us in political or social thinking and thereby play right into the hands of the Communists.

If you are tempted to join one of these anti-Communist organizations, resist the temptation.

Turn your zeal and your energy into positive action against Communism. Get rid of your frustrations by attacking the evils of segregation and discrimination. Prove to the rest of the world that democracy can work and Christianity can be lived to the fullest.

There are so many things you can do immediately:

1. Join or form a Catholic interracial council in your community.
2. Join and take an active part in the Urban League or the NAACP in your community.
3. Work for fair employment practices in your place of work; or announce that you are willing to hire Negroes for any job they are capable of, if you are in management.

4. Get acquainted with Negroes who are in the same profession with you.
5. Invite Negroes to your home and visit their homes.
6. Invite Negro couples into your C.F.M. or discussion group.
7. Find out what organizations in your community are working for fair housing, accommodations and employment practices and work with them.
8. Subscribe to and read a Negro publication, preferably a local one.
9. In your conversations, in your speeches, make others conscious of the racial problem.
10. Pray daily that Christ may love the Negroes in your community in and through you.

All this you can do as individuals. But the time has come for an all out, organized campaign by Catholic laymen against the evils of segregation and discrimination.

The race problem is a city problem, not a rural problem. Catholics live mostly in the cities. They are the largest and best organized group in all the major cities.

Who is in a better position to organize and lead a campaign for fair housing, accommodations and employment practices than we Catholics? Why have we held back so long? Of what are we afraid? We never lack courage when it comes to organizing against indecent literature. We have never worried much over what neighbors thought about our getting involved in such activities.

Our national councils of Catholic men and women have encouraged the indecent literature campaigns—even prepared promotional material for them. I challenge the national offices of these lay organizations to assist and promote similar campaigns against the evils of segregation and Protestant and Jewish neighbors will eagerly join us. Such campaigns must, of course, follow different patterns from that employed in the decent literature campaigns. These can be worked out with the cooperation of the National Catholic Conference for Interracial Justice.

What a rare opportunity this would be for the lay apostolate. Here is the work of the laymen in the Church, the work that only the laymen can do.

Do you remember seeing the picture in the newspapers several months ago of an Oklahoma priest who was arrested for taking part in a sit-in demonstration? The picture was not pretty. A Catholic priest, in black suit with Roman collar still in place, carried like a common criminal into a paddy wagon by two policemen, one pinioning his arms, the other hoisting his legs, ignominiously.

You may remember that Bishop Victor J. Reed, of Oklahoma City, came to the defense of his priest. In a public statement he said:

"It is the duty of the clergy to preach, to teach, and to form the consciences of the laity with respect to the civic and social implications of Christ's teaching on the dignity and equality of men. It is primarily the responsibility of the laity to see that these teachings are translated into our civic and social relations. In isolated and exceptional instances—and in the absence of sufficient lay activity—the clergy may take direct action in these matters."

Bishop Reed justified the action of his priest on the grounds that there were no Catholic laymen willing and prepared to do the job.

This was the work of the layman. This was work that should be a part of the lay apostolate. It is the layman who alone can make it possible for the Church to be the soul of society. His apostolate is not primarily to organize retreats and Holy Name breakfasts: his is the thrilling work of applying Christ's revolutionary teaching to society.

As Pope Pius XII said in 1946: "Today more than ever (the Church) must live her mission; more energetically than ever she must repulse that narrow and false conception of her spirituality and inward life which would confine her, blind and dumb, to the recesses of the sanctuary. . . . The faithful, more precisely the laity, are in the front line of the Church's life; through them, the Church is the vital principle of human society. Consequently, they particularly must have an ever more clear consciousness, not only of belonging to the Church, but of being the Church."

I challenge you laymen and women to be the Church today by bringing Christ's answer to the racial problem.

I should like to make the challenge specific. We are being brainwashed these days by television, magazines and newspapers with a maudlin, sentimental attempt to glorify the Civil War. The Civil War was not something glorious; it was something bloody, ugly and disgraceful; it was our punishment for enslaving the Negro. There is no point in recalling it at all except for the lessons we can learn from it.

I suggest that Catholic lay organizations keep in mind that on January 1, 1963, we shall mark the Centennial of the Emancipation Proclamation. The best way to observe that Centennial would be to prove dramatically to the world that the Negro in the United States is at last able to enjoy his emancipation to the fullest. That may be asking too much in such a short time.

I suggest that Catholic laymen and women, united in organizations and as individuals, dedicate themselves to solving the racial problem so that by 1963 Catholics in all our large cities will have led the way in making contributions to the elimination of segregation and discrimination that will be fitting memorials of the Emancipation Proclamation.

Let's approach this problem in the typical American way—with impatience, with a determination to get results, immediate results.

Session VI—Where Do We Find God?

OUTLINE   In the Universe
Story of the Young Man

HOMILY

Where do we find God? Perhaps we feel that it is easier to discover God in the grandeur of the universe. Astrophysicists have recently discovered two fascinating phenomena: mysterious segments in the universe called "black holes" and "white holes." They suggest that through these holes matter passes back and forth between our universe and others. They speculate that other universes may coexist with ours, in the same reality but on a different space-time dimension, with the holes as "transfer points." The grandeur of God was tremendous before, but now with the possibility of many other universes besides ours, it staggers our imagination. We see the greatness and wonder of creation.

But what about our notions of God? There is a story about a young man taken up into heaven. After a few days of sightseeing there he returned to his home town. Quickly he became the center of attention, answering all kinds of questions about what he had seen. One friend asked him: "What is God like?" His answer really blew their minds: "She is black." This is a pointed reminder that all of our ideas about God are merely concepts and inadequate.

This same point is brought out in the beautiful passage from 1 Kings 19 where Elijah is told that the Lord is going to pass by. Elijah goes out of the cave to see the Lord; he looks for him in the rock-splitting wind, in the earthquake, in the fire—but the Lord is not in any of these. Finally, Elijah hears a tiny whispering sound, he covers his face, for he found the Lord in the gentle breeze. In this tender and penetrating passage we are warned to distrust all our concepts about God, for God passes by in the most unexpected and quiet ways.

If each of us here were to give our concept of God, I am sure there would be many different descriptions.

—For some, God is the man on the mountain, the power in the bolt of lightning.

—For some, God is the Supreme Being, the Creator of the universe.

—For some, God is the mistaken idea, the holdover from another age.

—For some, God is the gentle word offered, the bread broken, the cup of wine shared.

—And for some, God is life, love, the hope-filled thought that tomorrow willbe better than today.

We have taken this word "god" and filled it with our ideas. Each concept of God has its truth, and each is inadequate.

It is a fact of modern life that God has become unreal for

many people. Note, for example, the problem of prayer. For many it is not whether prayers are answered or not, but whether there is anyone there to hear our prayers. Two men in this century who have spoken profoundly about the problem of believing were the Trappist Thomas Merton and the scientist-theologian Teilhard de Chardin. Merton pointed out that to say God is dead really means the customary symbols of God are dead due to a shift in world views. Chardin observed that our century was genuinely religious, but had not yet found the God it could adore.

Our images of God as the heavenly power who helps our ball team to win or the God who won't spoil the picnic by rain are inadequate. Leo Tolstoi said: "When the savage no longer believes in his wooden God, it does not mean there is no God. It means the true God is not made of wood." In our own lives the sun rises every morning, the winds blow, clouds race across the sky, white-caps chase each other across a lake, the aroma of barbecued steak reaches us, we are touched gently by someone we love. If we are too busy to take a few moments to experience such good things, we would not be very impressed by the goodness and power of God in some great miracle. The point of the passage from 1 Kings about the gentle breeze is that we find God in unexpected ways— everywhere.

We need this ability to see God everywhere. Teachers of severely retarded children tell of their amazement on seeing these usually blank faces light up with a smile, a sign of understanding. There is nothing more beautiful than seeing someone's face light up—the face of an old man, a stranger, an outcast who suddenly finds himself treated with respect and love. God shows himself in these faces.

Remember when you were engaged, in love, the joy you found in bringing a smile to your beloved's face. How long has it been now since you stopped transfiguring each other like that? Or remember how, when your children were little, you would attract their attention, make them smile? Now their expressions are often closed, and they pretend indifference. Do you think you can still work your power of transfiguration on them? The greatest revelations of God are all around us, especially in people. If you have brought about such a revelation through your love, then you know nothing can be more divine, you understand why God became a man. You then have a glimpse of God. You, as Elijah, have seen God in the gentle breeze.

Session VII—Levels of Communication

Outline

COMMUNE 1. Smallest division of local government
2. Verb:
   (a) to talk intimately
   (b) to receive Holy Communion

| **APPROACHES** | 1. Those without a God—meaning of life |
| | 2. Those with a God—meaning of life, constant prayer |

| **HARNACK** | Adolph von Harnack: "These people. . . ." |

LEVELS OF COMMUNICATION	1. Talk about things
	2. Talk about persons not present
	3. Past feelings—not present

ATMOSPHERE AND ATTITUDE	1. Super snooper
	2. Intellectual—you're interesting
	3. Penny psychologist—you're good
	4. Doom and gloom—healing

FEARS	1. Afraid to have people know us
	2. Fear of criticism or making a mistake
	3. Used against me
	4. Afraid of change
	5. Inferiority complex or hang-ups

CORRECTIONS

HOMILY

If you were to look up the word "commune" in the dictionary, it would give this word as a noun and as a verb. As a noun it is defined "as the smallest division of local government in France, Belgium, and other countries." But, as a verb it is given two meanings: 1. *to talk intimately*, and 2. to receive Holy Communion. This is going to be the theme of our retreat. Can we commune with others, with ourselves, and finally with God?

To commune really means to seek the very heart of all that is about us. For those without a God this communing brings them to the deepest relationship of the meaning of life. To those with a God it means the same thing, but also a constant prayer. We can say it is a constant prayer because a person then hears the voice of God in his fellowmen, in himself, and in this communing posture he is in prayer and can commune with his God.

The very nature of marriage is to speak intimately with one's spouse. It means to commune, or to have a communion in a sacramental form. Without this deep communion, a marriage loses its strong Christian meaning.

Perhaps the most obvious appreciation of this is in the symbol of the wedding ring. In ancient times, before Christ, people believed that the main nerve system began from the third finger, left or right hand. The use of the wedding ring was a symbol of embrace, that is, a symbol that the spouse embraced the very nerve center and very feeling core of his bride. Without speaking intimately, this symbol is worn in vain and the power of its extraordinary meaning deprives the couple of "the greatest amount of happiness known to man."

May I just say at the very beginning that this is a problem for all Christians, when our evolution of society with its transiency and hurry began to reveal how far we were being separated from each other. This appeared especially evident in religious life. Many who were unable to seek the communing with their fellow religious began to seek it elsewhere and eventually left the religious order, society or group to find it. Harnack, a German historian and biblical scholar, wrote of religious life in France: "There people come together without knowing each other, live together without loving each other, and die without knowing each other." This very harsh and horrifying comment on the style of life that might or might not have been extant in French religious life can also be a measurement of the Christian life abroad. It is something about which we really have to think. Without much challenge we might find some reflection of this in the style that was prevalent in many forms of religious worship. People came together to pray separately, not knowing or loving each other.

LEVELS OF COMMUNICATION

There are grades of communication among people. Each grade allows a person to enter into a relationship with another at different degrees.

7. To talk about things (cocktail party conversation: dogs, trips, operations).
6. To talk about the past feelings of two people not present.
5. To talk about the present feelings of people not present.
4. To talk about *my* past feelings for person not present.
3. To talk about my present feelings for a person not present.
2. To talk about my past feelings for a person who is present.
1. To talk about my present feelings for a person who is present.

The most powerful communion between individuals occurs in the last two. This is where individuals really begin to share each other's life. The Newman Club has a saying—"Cor Loquitur ad Cor"—which means "Heart Speaks to Heart." This has been the desire of mankind, and it is the richest manner of living.

Some months ago, Bill Coulson came to the Renewal Center as a guest speaker for one of our Dimension 70 Series. Bill is the man who is closely allied to Carl Rogers as a person and as a co-worker. When he came to our community, on the occasion of giving this talk, one of the brothers approached him and asked if he would talk to our own immediate community about friendliness, love, and communication. He felt that while we were doing so much for the Christian body at large, we were not really speaking to each other on very loving and caring terms. Bill said he would be very happy to meet with the community. So, this brother went around to the different members of the community saying that we would have a meeting Tuesday night at 10:00 with Bill Coulson. It was a comedy to see the different reactions among the members of the community when this challenge to "speak intimately" was presented to them. Two of the members refused outright, with varying excuses. Another member of the community immediately objected but then thought that perhaps we should venture into this. Another member of the community who had had some encounter experience thought that it was a magnificent idea. Another member of the community registered sheer horror, with the words, "Who, us?" But he, too, was willing to attend. On the night of the community meeting, we gathered together nervously. At the beginning it was slow. Finally, one of the members ventured out with a question. "What is the pain that is being felt in this community?" This unleashed an extraordinarily beautiful, intimate and caring two-hour session in which the community members spoke more deeply to each other than they had in two years of casual conversation.

COMMUNION WITH GOD

Of course we are very adjusted to think in terms of communion with our God through the Eucharist; however, that is only one form. There are many forms in which God communes with us and we with him. Perhaps the most powerful communion of God to us is through our fellowmen. This means that we have to be able to *accept correction.* The liturgies during September were particularly beautiful with regard to this factor of growth. Jesus said this to his disciples: "If your brother should commit some wrong against you, go and point out his faults. But keep it between the two of you. If he listens to you, you have won your brother over. If he does not listen, however, summon another so that every case may stand on the word of two or three witnesses. If he ignores them, refer to the Church. If he ignores the Church then treat him as you would a Gentile or a tax collector."

"Owe no debt to anyone except the debt that binds us to love one another. He who loves his neighbor has fulfilled the law" (Romans 13:8). The most powerful communion that we can have of personal growth is the personal exchange of one's value systems and revelations from God.

PEANUTS CARTOON

In one of the cartoons, Lucy, Charlie Brown and Linus are lying down on a mound and looking at the sky. Lucy says: "If you use your imagination you can see lots of things in the cloud formation. What do you think you see, Linus?" Linus: "Those clouds up there look to me like the map of the British Honduras and Caribbean. That cloud up there looks a little like the profile of Thomas Eakins, the famous painter and sculptor. And that group of clouds over there gives me the impression of the stoning of Steven. I can see the apostle Paul standing there on one side." Lucy: "Uh huh, that's very good. And what do you see in the clouds, Charlie Brown?" Charlie Brown: "Well, I was going to say that I saw a ducky and a horsey, but I changed my mind."

CONCLUSION

To commune, to speak intimately with another is in a true Christian sense to hear the voice of God and to understand the heart of people. In marriage, this is the very reason for the union. This is the sacrament of communion as it is lived out in the sacrament of marriage.

Session VIII—Joy

Outline

The History of Aesthetical Theology
    St. Teresa (The Big Flower)
    St. Francis of Assisi
    St. Thomas More
    St. Bernadette

Basic Theology
    God is attractive.
    Therefore religion should be attractive.

Physical and Psychological Results
    Psychologically—the harmony of body
    Absence of Psychological Tensions
    Psychological—a sense of well-being and harmony

Examples
    The boy training for the priesthood and the little girls— "happy talk"
    Dog with a happy ending

Philosophy—Joy: If you don't find it, you create it!
    Success is getting . . .
    Happiness is wanting . . .
    The Buckets
    The Prince
    Jesus said: "How can I say rejoice?"

HOMILY

AESTHETICAL THEOLOGY

There is a banner which very well expresses what I would like to treat in this talk. The banner says: "Joy Is the Infallible Sign of God's Presence."

St. Teresa of Avila once said: "From silly devotions and sour-faced saints deliver us." This pretty well indicates the tone of aesthetical theology.

St. Francis of Assisi once approached a very glum friar who seemed to believe that if he was going to be holy he had to be glum. St. Francis' reaction was: "Brother, why are you so glum? If you have sinned, go to confession and if you have not, then show the joy of God in your life."

St. Thomas More was certainly a beautiful example of a man

who walked with his God and as a consequence found joy in many of the severe crises of his life. He was a man with an eminent sense of humor. There are many examples in his life which bring this out. One in particular was when he was being led up the scaffolding where he was to be beheaded. His jailer was helping him. St. Thomas turned to him and said: "It is very nice of you to be helping me now, but perhaps you could save your energy for when I come down, then I will really need your help."

St. Bernadette was another example of a woman who, because of her presence of God, was able to keep a beautiful sense of humor with an immense amount of physical disorder. She was often asked to come down to recreation to enliven the atmosphere of the community.

BASIC THEOLOGY

If God is good, all-caring, and interested in us then he must be attractive. If God is attractive, religion must be attractive. Those who mirror depression and gloom are certainly not reflecting the presence of a beautiful God.

PHYSICALLY

It goes as an accepted fact among both the psychologists and the doctors that there is a great link between the psyche and the somatic. Many disorders and/or discomforts can be attributed to psychological problems. These are problems of the spirit which do not have the comfort of knowing the providence of God. Many of these disorders are often caused by the lack of an awareness of God and his peace.

PSYCHOLOGICAL EFFECTS

A person who is truly in tune with his God is a person who walks in joy and confidence. In one of the surveys which was done at a Chicago university it was found that "the most normal person" was a Christian who followed the teaching of his belief and realized God's care for him.

EXAMPLES

A. Some years ago a boy who was studying for the priesthood was faced with the problem of caring for his mother after his father had died. Though he was five years along in his study for the priesthood termination of his studies seemed inevitable. At this time the rector of the seminary said to him: "John, before you leave I want you to know that I am very sad to see you go. I have spent fifteen years of my life dedicated to the training of these students for the priesthood but sometimes I have often wondered whether you have done more good than I. Oftentimes when a boy was homesick or discouraged I sent him to you just to talk. Your vibrance, your joy, your enthusiasm have been the cause of many of the boys here continuing on in their pursuit of the priesthood. I want to commend you for this, and God willing this will be a continued witness of yours as a priest."

B. One time a little girl went to a party where all the people who were older were talking about their dogs, operations, and trips. The little girl thought that the conversation was very gloomy.

Her only remark to her mother was: "Mama, can't we go someplace where people have happy talk?"

C. One time a little girl was promised by her father, who was very adverse to having animals around the house, that she could have a pet on her tenth birthday. When the day arrived she reminded her father of the promise. They went down to the pet shop and were shown the parrakeets, a monkey in a cage, kittens, and all the other assortment of animals. Finally, they came to a bin that contained puppies. The puppies were jumping all over each other and in their playful way they were having all the activity possible. In the corner one kept wagging his tail and playing with the other puppies. Finally, the little girl was asked by her father: "Honey, which one is it going to be?" She pointed to the puppy in the corner. "I'll take that one with the happy ending!"

BASIC PHILOSOPHY

There is a saying which is printed on some of the signs sold in art shops. It gives pretty much the basic philosophy of anyone who is in pursuit of joy. It says: "Happiness and joy are things that you do not find; you make them. Success is getting what you want; happiness is wanting what you get."

One of the ancient proverbs talks about two buckets who were sitting on the edge of the well, commenting on their state in life. One bucket said: "I always find myself empty. I leave here full and come back empty. It is such a depressing life." The other bucket said: "Isn't that unique? I always find myself filled. I leave here filled and come back here to be filled again."

One of the stories that is often found in children's readers is the one about the prince who was seeking happiness. One day he rode out to the countryside and there against the hill he saw a shepherd tending his flock. He rode over and found a boy in ragged clothes who was playing a flute. He asked the boy why he was so happy. Beaming, the boy, who did not know the status of his visitor, said to the prince: "Why should I be anything other than happy? Could anyone, even the king or the queen, or the princess or the prince be more favored than I. I have the sky to look at; I have my flocks to care for; I have the fresh air, the moisture of the grass, the ruggedness of the rocks, the beauty of the countryside. Who could be more blessed than I." And the prince answered: "I guess it is because you see all the beauty of our land that you are happy."

Those who see the beauty of their land, the dignity of their person, the magnificence of their call as Christians are able to say with true meaning: "Life is a joy." If you take the words of Jesus and substitute for "peace" its synonym "joy," you will find the message of the master to be very strong. At his birth the angels sang of the joy to man. The words of Jesus in his final address to his people were: "My peace (joy) I leave you, my peace (joy) I give you." This allowed one of the great Christians to exclaim: "Rejoice, again I say rejoice!"

Joy is the infallible sign of God's presence!

Outline

CARDINAL SUENENS: "WHY ARE YOU A MAN OF HOPE?"
THE THEOLOGICAL VIRTUES
ABBA FATHER
   Example: My daddy is the conductor.
THE IMPOSSIBLE DREAM
DIRECTIVES FOR YOUTH FORMATION
   A world filled with murders, marriage disasters, six million
   Jews annihilated, newscasts, etc.
JESUS' CONCEPT
GROOVY

HOMILY

  Some time ago Cardinal Suenens visited the Franciscan Renewal Center in Scottsdale, Arizona. The staff, which had often used his letter—"Why Are You a Man of Hope Even in These Days?"—mentioned to him how pleased they were with his writing. He then discussed the background for the writing of this beautiful epistle. He said that he was being interviewed by some of the press at one of his lectures. One of the reporters was so impressed by his optimism that he asked him why he was a man of hope. The cardinal at that time was on his way out of the airport to catch a flight to his next destination. He quickly took the man's name and told him that he would write him an answer. He left on his flight, reached his destination, and was taken to a hotel. That night he wrote out the first and only draft of his letter.

WHY ARE YOU A MAN OF HOPE EVEN IN THESE DAYS?

Because I believe that God is new every morning, I believe that God is creating the world today, at this very moment. He did not just create it in the long ago and then forget about it. That means that we have to expect the unexpected as the normal way God's Providence is at work.

That "unexpected" of God is exactly what saves and liberates us from determinism and from the sociologism of gloomy statistics about the state of human affairs in the present. That "unexpected," since it comes from God, is something coming out of his love for us, for the betterment of his children.

I am hopeful, not for human reasons or because I am optimistic by nature, but because I believe in the Holy Spirit present in his Church and in the world—even if people don't know his name. I am hopeful because I believe that the Holy Spirit is still the creating Spirit, and that he will give us every morning fresh freedom, joy and a new provision of hope, if we open our souls to him.

The story of the Church is a long story, filled with the wonders of the Holy Spirit: We must remember the saints and the prophets bringing, in hopeless times, a gulf stream of graces and new lights to continue on the road.

I believe in the surprises of the Holy Spirit. The Council was such a surprise, and Pope John was another. They took us aback. Why should we think that God's imagination and love might be exhausted?

Hope is a duty, not just a nicety. Hope is a dream, but a way of making dreams become reality.

Happy those who dream dreams and are ready to pay the price to make them come true!

THE THEOLOGICAL VIRTUES

I have a great difficulty trying to distinguish the theological virtues in the categories commonly given as faith, hope, and love. To me a person who falls in love has all the theological virtues of faith, hope, and love. If a person is in love, hope is a very strong quality of his being. For instance, take a person who is now engaged to be married. This person has hope, many times, to a fault. The world is filled with possibilities. The world is an impossible dream. Similarly, a woman who is now pregnant because of love has hope to an immeasurable degree. There are people who plan the future of the unknown with great expectancy and concrete expressions of that hope.

THEOLOGY

This is very evident in the writings of the early Christian people. They were people who were being knocked down but not knocked out. They were people who would be killed but would not lose life. There is just an unusual amount of hope in their expression of the presence of Jesus among them. There was an expectance, a pregnancy that allowed them to see life with a vision far beyond that of those who did not have a resurrection destiny. This is again referred to in the epistles with a simple Aramaic expression of "Abba Father." This is the babbling of a child who coos in the hands or the presence of his father.

THE SECULAR PHILOSOPHY

Oftentimes a type of hope is suggested to the people in the songs of the nation. Such examples that come to my mind immediately are "You'll Never Walk Alone" from *Carousel* and "The Impossible Dream" from *Man of La Mancha*. Something has often puzzled me in the latter case: Of what does "the unreachable star" really consist? The big question that comes to my mind is what *is* the unreachable star? Is it money, fame, material things? For the Christian, the impossible dream or the unreachable star would be Jesus. If the words of that song are sung or said with this in mind, for the Christian this is an unusual enunciation. The greatness of the Christian hope!

DIRECTIVES FOR YOUTH FORMATION

A couple of years ago the communications bureau for youth responded to the atmosphere that was so prevalent among the youth and even among the adults of our age. It stated that if anyone were going to do anything for the youth of today, these individuals would have to respond to the terrible fatalism that existed among the youth. Or, to put it more concretely, if they were going to uplift the young people of our nation, they would have to give them a sense of hope. It was mentioned that all the communications media emphasized the reporting of murders, divorces, the memory of the annihilation of six million Jews and the sense of fatalism that many young people felt toward Vietnam. To give a sense of hope to a stricken people would be the greatest contribution any educator, speaker or youth leader could ever give to his group and to his nation.

GROOVY   A couple of years ago in the psychiatric ward of O'Connor Hospital a man was admitted who had the heavy lines of despair upon his face and upon his attitude toward life. He was a man who had a weak heart, and his attitude toward life of doom and gloom from womb to tomb was fatalistic. Present in the department was a young nurse with a wonderful sense of humor and hope. It was very obvious to the department psychiatrist that if anyone could do this man any good it was the young nurse. So he assigned the gloomy man to the young nurse. She played checkers, ping pong, pinochle, and other games with him. The happy word of the time was "groovy." He often mentioned when he scored a point that the appropriate word for joy would be groovy. She tried to get him to say this again and again. He refused to do this. A short time later the gloomy man had a heart attack. He was rushed to intensive care. The young nurse had learned to love this depressed man. During her lunch hour, before and after work, she went to visit him. Fortunately, she was there when he regained consciousness. When he opened his eyes and saw her standing there his response was "groovy!"

This kind of hope should be animatedly present in Christians today. These are the people who are witness to one of the greatest God-like virtues present among man—hope—"I am hopeful, not for human reasons or because I am optimistic by nature, but because I believe in the Holy Spirit present in his Church and in the world."

Session X—Commitment in Marriage

Outline

CARL ROGERS—FREEDOM AND COMMITMENT
COMMITMENT IS . . .
DESIRE TO BRING LOVE TO MARRIAGE
VISIT WITH CHAPLAIN
PSYCHE AND SOMA
WANTING TO LIVE
TO DECIDE IS NOT TO DECIDE

CARL ROGERS—LACK OF COMMITMENT
PLAYING BALL
LOW MOMENTS OF MARRIAGE
IMPOSSIBLE DREAM
SPARK OF LIFE

HOMILY

Carl Rogers has written in his book, *Freedom and Commitment*, some very insightful and beautiful passages. I really believe that he addresses himself to one of the critical issues of our times when he writes:

"Certainly the disease of our age is the lack of purpose, the lack of meaning, the lack of commitment on the part of individuals. Is there anything that I can say in this regard other than that it is clear to me that in therapy as indicated in the examples that I have given, commitment to purpose and to meaning in life is one of the significant elements of change? It is only when a person declares "I am someone . . . I am someone worth being . . . I am committed to being myself" that change becomes possible.

Commitment is a total organismic direction, involving not only the conscious mind but the whole direction of the organism itself. In my judgment, commitment is something one discovers within himself.

"Commitment is more than a decision. Man is most successful in a commitment when he is functioning as an integrated, whole, unified individual. The more that he is functioning in this total manner, the more confidence he has in the direction which he unconsciously chooses."

There is one thing that a therapist, a marriage counselor, or whoever, is unable to affect within a person. That is the desire to make something work, to affect a healthy change, to bring about love in a marriage. This has to be a desire that comes from within. Jesus said: "The kingdom of God is *within*." There is an old cliché that says: "God helps those who help themselves." Have you ever thought of the alternative to that slogan? The alternative would be: "God cannot help those who do not want to help themselves."

Today, there is a very prominent saying: "If man wants to live, he must say, 'Yes' to life."

About a year ago, I was helping on one of the military bases and I walked into the chaplain's office before a conference. He told me to sit down and then he narrated an experience that he had just had a few hours before. He told me the story that when he was in Korea, he was passing one of the field tent hospitals when one of the doctors came out and said: "Father, you had better go in and take care of that young lad. He is really shot up and I don't think he will live." So the priest said that he went into the tent and walked to the side of the boy. He looked down at the boy who was in pain and said to him: "Son, is there anything that you would like me to tell your mother or your wife, or any of your family?" The boy looked at him, and with some pain he asked the priest to reach inside of his jacket. The priest obliged and pulled out a very thin wallet, within which were a few pictures and a $10 bill. The priest asked him what he wanted him to do with it. Again in a halting voice, the boy said: "I'll bet you the $10 bill that I pull through." The priest immediately responded by saying: "You're on, son." With that, he anointed him and shortly afterward, left. Four years later, a GI knocked at the chaplain's door at Fort Ord. The chaplain called for him to enter, and the boy came in limping somewhat and announced: "You owe me $10." The priest, in utter surprise, asked the normal question: "What for?" The boy recalled the incident in Korea and announced that he was that man and he wanted his $10. The priest gladly gave him the amount of the bet and congratulated him on his determination to live.

I see many, many parallels between the psyche (spirit) and the soma (body). There are numerous cases in the medical field in which a person was not supposed to live, but because of an interior spark for life the person lived. This same thing is repeated again and again in marriage contracts. There are times when it seems as though death is imminent within a marriage, but because of the determination, that spirit to live and to love, the marriage does survive. In many cases, it survives with the pair involved experiencing a great luster and a strong compassion for each other. This is that infallible "yes" to live out a promise.

There is no priest, no counselor, no psychiatrist, who can make a person grow or live. The individual himself or herself must want to live, must want to grow, must want to love. This is the grace of life and that quality which makes a person beautiful. Identical twins can live the exact same life in the exact same circumstances, yet while one cries about his plight and is non-productive, the other is vibrant and ever-growing. That is the spark to live and to live well. That is the "yes" to live out a commitment, a vocation, a "yes" to holiness, a "yes" to life, a "yes" to love, the "yes" of commitment.

There is a rather popular poster that says: "To decide is not to decide." Translated into my vernacular, it means that to want to live is to live. To want to die is to die. That certain something that makes a person beautiful and a success in every circumstance is the commitment to fulfill a vocation.

This cannot be toyed with. Married couples who chant divorce or separation at low moments in their marriage are people who are halfhearted in their commitment. There is no question that, in our times, this chant of easy termination of a marriage is popular. But a person who is committed responds to what is truth, not to what is popular.

Again, Carl Rogers addresses himself to what commitment or the lack of commitment will produce against the pressures outside.

"Let me describe another psychological experiment done by Dr. Richard Crutchfield in California (1955), which again illustrates the way in which behavior may be controlled so that it appears the individual is unfree. In this experiment five subjects at a time are seated side by side—each in an individual booth screened from the other. Each booth has a panel with various switches and lights. The subject can use the switches to signal his judgment on items that are projected on the wall in front of the group. The lights are signal lights which indicate what the other four members are giving to the item. The subjects are told that they will be given identifying letters, A, B, C, D, and E, and are instructed to respond, one at a time, in that order; however, when they enter the cubicles, each discovers that he is letter E. They are not permitted to talk during the session.

"Actually, the lights in each booth are controlled by the experimenter and do not express the judgment of the other four members. Thus, on those critical items where the experimenter wishes to impose group pressure, he can make it appear that all four members, A through D, agree on an answer which is clearly at variance with the correct answer. In this way, each subject is confronted with a conflict between his own judgment and what he believes to be the consensus of the group. Thus, for example, the question may be: 'Which of these two irregular figures is larger—X or Y?' The individual sees clearly that X is larger than Y, yet one after another the lights flash on indicating that all the other four members regard Y as being the larger figure. Now it is his turn to decide. How will he respond? Which switch will he press? Crutchfield has shown that, given the right conditions, almost everyone will desert the evidence of his senses or his own honest opinions and conform to the seeming consensus of the group. For example, some high level mathematicians yielded to the false group consensus on some fairly easy arithmetic problems, giving wrong answers that they would never have given under normal circumstances."

There is no doubt that depression is one of the obvious qualities of many people today. But do you know what depression is? Do you know the feeling? Do you know what causes depression? The definition given in psychology for depression, at least one of the definitions, is "anger at one's self for not doing what the whole system knows it should do."

Let me give you an example. If I am inside, watching a group of my peers playing ball and having a joyous time outside in the yard, and I want to join them, I know I should join them, and I need this recreation, but if I do not open the door and walk out, I am going to be depressed. There is no other way that my whole organism is going to react, because I know that I could accomplish and participate in this joy.

In marriage, one or the other individual often becomes depressed. In my opinion, this is a result of being locked in on only one solution. At the present time, the other party will not communicate or respond the way the other wishes. Instead of seeking other solutions, even of self-development during the time of lull, impatiently and in an exasperating manner, they force the one solution that is most apparent to them at the moment. This may well be doomed to failure. If people are committed, they will seek other solutions. They will try other ways of accomplishing a given vocation or goal. This is the beauty of a commitment.

There are many songs and sayings that want to encourage a person to commitment. You're familiar with the words to a song from the play *Carousel*: "When you walk through a storm, keep your head up high and don't be afraid. . . ." There is another beautiful song that speaks well to the sickness of our time, the lack of commitment. It is from the musical *Man of La Mancha*. That song is entitled "The Impossible Dream."

There is a spark of life that determines so very much in all phases of existence, and this is true in the success of a marriage. That spark of life has to come from within. That is the Kingdom of God. This, no one can give you. This spark of life you have to develop within yourself. You have to have the courage of accomplishing the beautiful, the sublime, and the loving. This makes the so-called "impossible marriages" operable. It makes the ordinary marriage beautiful. It makes the good marriage sublime. And to this, God, and all of life, calls you.

IV. FILMS

by Mario DiCicco, O.F.M.

A. INTRODUCTION

The following is a beginner's library of creative short films which can be shown in the context of a retreat that reflects on the natural and supernatural co-dimensions of man. They are artistic films and so require active participation by the viewer and imaginative handling by the discussion leader. In other words, the output will be commensurate with the input. There are a few practical considerations to be made here:

1. Before you order the films from the companies listed, be sure to check with the public city and county libraries to see if they have the films in their own collection. Most large cities, and even some small towns which act as regional libraries, have a marvelous collection of films. Also check with your respective diocesan office of religious education. Some dioceses have very fine audiovisual departments. This will save you a lot of money, since the films in these places are either free or else loaned for a small insurance fee.

2. When ordering your films from the companies listed, be sure to consider the postage both ways in the price indicated. Sometimes the postage can come to about $3 over the rental price of the film.

3. If you plan to use films on your retreat, it would be wise to order them well in advance, so that you can have them on the dates you want to screen them. In scheduling, here is something to consider: most companies send you the films two days, sometimes a week before the show date, certainly by the day before. However, in practically all cases, the film companies insist that you have the film postmarked the very next day after the show date and sent back immediately. If you don't, you will inconvenience the next person who intends to use the film.

4. Two or three of the films listed have no film distributor indicated. This information was not readily available. It is suggested that you write to one of the main film distributors, such as Contemporary, and ask them for the distributor.

5. It goes without saying that the discussion leader should preview the film before showing it to the group so that he can draw up significant questions for fruitful interaction. In the films given here, there are possible avenues of discussion suggested.

The impact of a film to stir deep personal reflection on

some of the profound questions of life is an evident truth today. God's revelation comes to man in many ways: through a dream, from a burning bush, by means of a vision in the sky. He also speaks through the film, sometimes so powerfully to the sensitive, open viewer that, like the book that inspired St. Ignatius of Loyola to follow Christ, this medium can challenge one to intense encounter with one's self, with the world, and with the Lord.

B. FILM DISTRIBUTORS

McGRAW HILL/CONTEMPORARY
FILMS
828 Custer Avenue
Evanston, Illinois 60602
(or) Princeton Road
      Heightstown, New Jersey 08520
(or) 1714 Stockton Street
      San Francisco, Calif. 94133

MASS MEDIA MINISTRIES
2116 North Charles Street
Baltimore, Maryland 21218
(or) 1714 Stockton Street
      San Francisco, Calif. 94133

ROA FILMS
1696 North Astor Street
Milwaukee, Wisconsin 53202

CINE-CATH
Catholic Missions
371 Fifth Street
Manistee, Michigan 49660

NBC EDUCATIONAL ENTERPRISES
30 Rockefeller Plaza
New York, New York 10020

AUDIO/BRANDON
1616 North Cherokee
Los Angeles, Calif. 90028
(or) 512 Burlington Avenue
      La Grange, Illinois 60525
(or) 34 MacQuesten Parkway So.
      Mount Vernon, New York 10550

FRANCISCAN COMMUNICATIONS
CENTER
TeleKETICS Division
1229 South Santee Street
Los Angeles, Calif. 90015

PUBLIC RELATIONS OFFICE
3140 Merimec Street
Saint Louis, Missouri 63118

PYRAMID FILMS
Box 1048
Santa Monica, Calif. 90406

STEPHEN BOSUSTOW
PRODUCTIONS
20548 Pacific Coast Highway
Malibu, Calif. 90265

CENTRON EDUCATIONAL FILMS
1621 West Ninth Street
Lawrence, Kansas 66044

CCM FILMS
866 Third Avenue
New York, New York 10022

UNIVERSITY OF ARIZONA
Bureau of A-V Services
Tucson, Arizona 85721

BOSTON UNIVERSITY
School of Education
Krasker Memorial Film Library
765 Commonwealth Avenue
Boston, Mass. 02215

UNIVERSITY OF ILLINOIS
Visual Aid Services
Champaign, Illinois 61820

UNIVERSITY OF MICHIGAN
A-V Education Center
Ann Arbor, Michigan

UNIVERSITY OF MINNESOTA
Dept. of A-V Extension
2037 University Avenue, S.E.
Minneapolis, Minn. 55455

UNIVERSITY OF MISSOURI
Extension Division
A-V and Communication Services
119 Whitten Hall
Columbia, Missouri 65201

FLORIDA STATE UNIVERSITY
Educational Media Center
Tallahassee, Florida 32306

UNIVERSITY OF SOUTHERN
CALIFORNIA
Film Distribution Section
Department of Cinema
University Park
Los Angeles, Calif. 90007

HARTLEY PRODUCTIONS
279 East 44th Street
New York, New York 10017

C. SUMMARIES

I. *NIGHT AND FOG*

This is an overpowering, brutally honest, disturbingly shocking film about the grim universe of the German concentration camps during World War II in which an incredible ten million people were reduced to sub-humanness, and finally and literally to ashes. Considered one of the twenty-five greatest films ever made, Alan Resnais' masterpiece communicates more of a visual and moral realization than it does an historical fact; and the perceptive viewer must transcend, as the film does, the factual dimensions of documentary and discover relentless suffering raised to the dignity of tragedy. The almost soothing music of Hans Eisler, the grim, laconic commentary of Jean Cayrol in French with English sub-titles, the raw footage in black and white alternating with color shots of the present mesh together, in a tense counterpoint of understatement, irony, and horrendous declaratve fact, the piercing and compelling account of a way of life, so easily erased, that it becomes a warning for the future.

The film begins with the history of the concentration camps and proceeds to show the inhuman conditions, the starvation, the disease, the despair, the "experimental" laboratories where human beings became guinea pigs, and finally, the gas chambers. The camera follows the victims, in actual captured black and white film, from the trains, where many died, to the "shower" rooms where millions died, its ceiling (now shown in color) full of torn concrete dug into by fingernails, a mute testimony to unparalleled evil. The final scenes, unbearable in any other context but visually necessary here, show great piles of clothing, mountains of hair, heaps of human skin, pits of hundreds of human bodies grotesquely littered, knotted, and sprawled. The next scene is fraught with outrage and almost insufferable irony, as a *kapo* (a guard), a soldier and an officer tell the courts, "I am not responsible." The narrator simply asks: "Then who is responsible?"

The effect of the first showing of *Night and Fog* is so overwhelming that no discussion should be held. One should be allowed to sit or walk in silence and reflect on the film's reality and realization. A second showing should be arranged, after which there is an exchange of accumulated feelings. The themes and questions are numerous: freedom, suffering, passive acquiescence to a criminal, decadent government, human dignity, personal responsibility for evil, violence, genocide (still a contemporary happening), war. How are we involved in the statement of the film? When does personal security become criminal? And, where were the Christians and their concerted voices in the midst of this official outrage? The final commentary of the film sums up the ambiguity of mass barbarism and the ease with which men prefer to ignore their scars and the lessons of history:

> . . . there are those of us who sincerely look upon the ruins today, as if the old concentration camp monster were dead and buried beneath them. There are those of us who pretend to take hope again as the image fades, as though there were a cure for the plague of these camps. There are those of us who pretend to believe that all this happened only once, at a certain time and in a certain place, and there are those of us who refuse to see, who do not hear the cry to the end of time.

To supplement one's experience of this film, one should read Viktor Frankl's powerful account of his own experiences in a Nazi concentration camp in his famous book, *Man's Search for Meaning*. Peter Weiss' play, *The Investigation*, which could be read or acted out in parts, is theater of fact and history, implausible in any other mode.

31 minutes

Contemporary Films

II. *A CHAIRY TALE*

This thoroughly provocative film created by Norman McLaren enacts a modern fable of interpersonal relations between a young man dressed in white and an ordinary kitchen chair. Done in ballet and pantomime with background music by the Indian musicians Ravi Shankar and Chatur Lal, the film opens with a young man walking on stage reading a book and abstractedly attempting to sit in a chair. Suddenly, the chair jerks away from him. He tries again, and the chair eludes him again, refusing to let the man sit down. The man chases after the chair which manages to escape him each time. A struggle ensues in which the man tries to master the chair. When this does not work, he reconciles himself to sitting on the floor, maintaining an air of indifference toward the chair, which approaches the man and nudges him for attention. The man tries understanding by tickling the chair, playing with it, dancing with it. Still the chair will not let the man sit in it. Finally, it dawns on the man that the chair wants to be treated as an equal and only when the man allows the chair to sit in his lap does it give itself completely to him.

The film says something very important about human relationships, how respect and reverence for another must inform one's every encounter. As Norman McLaren, the filmmaker, has said: "It involves a generalized human situation, makes a comment on the behavior of one human being to another, although the other human being is a chair." It is interesting to follow the man's approach to the chair. He treats it as an object. He takes it for granted, uses it mechanically, tries to dominate it by force, acts indifferently toward it, shows well-intentioned but deplorable lack of understanding and accurate empathy. Only when the man has reached the point of Buber's I-Thou relationship toward the chair does the chair accept the man totally. The man has surrendered his egocentricity and given witness to the mysteriousness of the other. He has finally heard the other's plea for community. He has gone beyond a mere instrumental approach and achieved sacramental awareness that the other is a unique and total being.

10 minutes

Contemporary	$5.00
Mass Media Ministries	$5.00
ROA Films	$5.00
Univ. of Arizona	$1.00
Boston Univ.	$5.00
Univ. of California	$5.00
Florida State Univ.	$2.50
Univ. of Illinois	$2.60
Univ. of Michigan	$2.25
Univ. of Minnesota	$2.00

III. *HUNGER IN AMERICA*

This CBS News Special Report is almost too much to take, so shocking are the scenes and facts, so poignant the suffering, so profound the irony, so hopeless the government relief programs. The film has been shown in Congress, and one senator commented that it ought to be shown in every classroom.

It is hard to believe that in this richest country in the world, with over $800 billion a year in production, as the documentary states, over 30 million out of 200 million Americans live in poverty, and 10 million live in a state of constant hunger. The CBS report examines four poverty areas in the United States: the Mexican population in San Antonio, Texas; the tenant farmer families in Louden County, Virginia; the Navajo Indians in the deserts of Arizona; and the Negroes of Alabama. The pictures and the comments from the poor and hungry themselves, from social workers and doctors, all hammer home the inescapable and maddening conclusion—slow starvation has become a way of life for millions of Americans. The horrible specter of hunger in a country which weekly slaughters and buries thousands of hogs because there is no market takes its toll in brain damage, malnutrition, marasmus, and ultimately death. And when the viewer realizes that more than 70 percent of this country's tax money goes to pay for past, present and future wars while less than 10 percent goes for health, labor, and welfare, and when the viewer further hears from Charles Kuralt, the film's narrator, that $400 million budgeted for relief food in 1967 was returned to the Treasury because of claims from the Department of Agriculture that existing programs didn't need the money, it is no wonder that this CBS report was considered one of the most startling presentations ever made on television.

This film has such impact on the viewer that discussion afterward is hardly needed. Everything is already said in the hopeless comments of the emaciated faces and listless bodies, in the pictures of babies with withered skin who die at age one, weighing five pounds, in the shameful statements of certain politicians. The film gnaws—like hunger.

52 minutes

Mass Media Ministries	$20.00
ROA Films	$17.50
Univ. of Minnesota	$13.80

IV. *THE DETACHED AMERICANS*

This CBS documentary, narrated by Harry Reasoner, was prompted by the shocking slaying of Kitty Genovese while 38 citizens watched from their windows without lifting a finger—not even a telephone receiver—to help. Incredible as it may seem, the murderer later admitted that he *figured* nobody would come to her aid. No one wanted to get involved, as many later confessed. "When she called to one she knew," the narrator says, "he never answered her. When it was all over, they (the spectators) all went back to bed."

The film proceeds, in an often heavily preachy but provocative way, to take a frank look at the disturbing elements of apathy, social irresponsibility, interpersonal disregard, and plain unconcern evident in American society today. In rapid sequence, the film investigates the reasons for such detached impersonalism, such as a loss of individuality and sense of identity, a feeling of isolation, role-playing and parallel living in a society which prizes means over ends, schooling over learning, property values over personal dignity, and striving over sharing. In scenes that are alternately satirical, tragic, and pathetic, the film tries to seek the root causes of this malaise in community, career, and home.

This film has not failed yet to provoke a lively and lengthy discussion on so many Christian values that seek to root out the self-centeredness, the defensive, minimal concern, the detachment and neutrality in everyone's life. The viewer finds himself asking, with regard to the stabbing death, "What would I have done in that case?" In a very real way, Christ's "Greater love than this no man has, that a man lay down his life for his friend" becomes a living challenge to the cautious and casual Christian whose detachment in so many less dramatic ways might be just as criminal. Harry Reasoner's comment in the film touches upon one of the great paradoxical teachings of the Gospel: "But if we do not give such lives as we have, do we live at all? What is life worth if we do not give it away?"

33 minutes

Mass Media Ministries $10.00
ROA Films $10.00
Univ. of Arizona $ 3.00
Univ. of California $ 8.50
Univ. of Minnesota $ 5.00
Univ. of Missouri $ 5.50

V. *THE RED BALLOON*

This French film, entirely without dialogue, is a classic of fantasy and childhood which tells the simple story of a small boy who "tames" a magnificent red balloon, which becomes his constant companion. It follows him to school, church, home. A gang of rough boys sees the young lad with the balloon and tries to snatch it from him, but the boy eludes them. Later they lie in wait for him and finally grab the balloon and destroy it. It becomes a shapeless red scrap. Suddenly, balloons from all over Paris snap loose everywhere, converge on the young boy and carry him away high over the city of Paris.

This film can spark numerous feelings and observations about love, friendship, human relationships. The way the red balloon responds to the young boy's delicate openness to its own individually distinctive beauty and allows itself to be tamed inspires thoughtful reflection on awareness, sensitivity, wonder, imagination. The logical, fussy, institutionalized behavior of the adults in the film, on the one hand, and the rough-minded, dirty boys, who become human counterparts of the drab Paris streets, on the other hand, contrast sharply with the free, open, bright spirit of the young boy in perfect harmony with the universe who weeps at the death of his balloon, at the death of beauty, but who is carried out of this world into a land where there is no brutish behavior or rigidity of spirit.

The film is enthralling and is an allegory open to many interpretations. One should read Antoine de Saint-Exupery's *The Little Prince* in conjunction with this film, where a fox teaches the little prince that "one only understands the things that one tames" and that "it is only with the heart that one can see rightly; what is essential is invisible to the eye. . . You become responsible, forever, for what you have tamed." The statement of Jesus—"Unless you become as little children, you cannot enter the kingdom of heaven"—also finds an echo in *The Red Balloon* and in the remark of the little prince that "only the children know what they are looking for."

45 minutes

Brandon Films
CCM Films $27.50

VI. *IS IT ALWAYS RIGHT TO BE RIGHT?*

This is a fast-moving parable, narrated by Orson Welles, which highlights the centers of divisiveness in our society—the generation gap, poverty, war, and racism. Why do people argue, ignore, hate, even kill one another? In brilliant color animation, often grotesquely humorous, the film tells of a land "where men were always right." When differences arise among the people, each side stands firm in its rightness—until one day, all activity stops. From this stalemate a tentative voice is heard to say: "I may be wrong. You may be right." At first the people are shocked to hear someone so cowardly and weak. But as they begin to listen, they see common beliefs in those that they have known only as adversaries. As communication between opposing groups increases, bright examples of joint action are seen in the land. The people state their faith in one another in a declaration of interdependence. They learn that the search for truth is never over, that the challenge is always the same—to stop long enough to listen, to learn, and to keep at a task that never ends.

The film is outstanding for provoking a lively discussion on listening, dialogue, and communication, the mutuality between learning as well as teaching, listening as well as telling. Why do discords arise between a husband and wife, between friends, between parent and child? Is it possible to resolve a bitter feud, dig up a buried hate, come to an honorable peace? The film explores the possibilities of an answer, not only in the title but in a declaration which is difficult for some people to make: "I may be wrong."

For true dialogical encounter, as Paolo Freire has written in his powerful book, *Pedagogy of the Oppressed*, love, humility, faith, and hope are needed. Dialogue cannot exist in the absence of a profound love for the world and for men, a love that is neither manipulative nor sentimental. Dialogue cannot exist without humility, for how can one dialogue if he always projects ignorance onto others and never perceives his own? Dialogue further requires "an intense faith in man, faith in his power to make and remake, to create and re-create, faith in his vocation to be more fully human." And lastly, dialogue cannot exist without hope, a hope "rooted in men's incompletion, from which they move out in constant search—a search which can be carried out only in communication with other men." With these qualities, then, dialogue becomes a horizontal relationship built on mutual trust.

8 minutes Stephen Bosustow Productions $25.00

VII. *ADVENTURES OF AN ASTERISK*

This sprightly animated film is the work of famous cartoonist, John Hubley, and is fully titled, *Adventures of an Asterisk, Where He Loves To Play and Enjoys Each New Thing He Sees— Unlike His Father—Who Has Forgotten How To Play and How To See New Things.*

The contrast from the beginning is between the imaginative, creative, alive, sensitive * (asterisk), and his dull father who is content to read the newspaper. The small * does everything the uninhibited child is accustomed to do: explore, imitate, create, wonder. One day he builds a tree house out of material from the pathway in front of his house. When his father, tired and worn, comes home from work and sees what has happened, he tears the tree house down and sends the small child off in tears.

Years pass and the small * becomes a man himself, having finished his education and settled down to a job and home of his own. He has a child * of his own who, like every child, wants to explore and create, but the father is at first disturbed and disinterested in his child's creation, a large play-horse made of scrap material. Finally, remembering his own youth, he decides to help. The horse becomes magically alive and both father and son ride off to a land of enchantment.

The imaginative cartoon says a lot about the ability to live joyously and creatively in the world, the fine art of letting go in the best sense of the word. It causes one to reflect honestly on the mindlessness in conformity and the totally unnecessary suppression of wonder, which inculcate needless anxiety and mediocrity. The office scene in which the grown-up * goes about his work joyously until his co-workers sniff and glower at his out-of-tuneness, causing him to slump like the rest, is a trenchant commentary on the quality of contemporary existence which looks at life as a problem to be solved through gritted teeth. Excitement, wonder, exploration, awareness, magic, naturalness, and openness —these are the child-like qualities a logical and technological society needs; and one senses that the Lord himself praised and prized the children for those very reasons, when he said of them to the grown-up apostles who were trying to be too bureaucratic and organized: "Let them be. Of such is the Kingdom!"

10 minutes

Contemporary Films	$12.50
Mass Media Ministries	$10.00
ROA	$10.00
Boston Univ.	$ 5.00
Univ. of California	$ 8.00
Florida State Univ.	$ 8.00
Univ. of Illinois	$ 4.05
Univ. of Missouri	$ 3.25

VIII. *THE SIXTIES*

This film is a model of the documentary-montage done by Charles Braverman in kinestatic technique (animation of still photographs through very fast cutting; known also as flash-frame technique) and newsreel clips of varying lengths. It is an exciting, visceral experience of the passions and polarities of a decade that witnessed the death of the two Kennedys and Martin Luther King, the rise of the Beatles and the Berlin Wall, the fight in Berkeley and the flight to the moon, the brutality in Vietnam, Biafra, and Selma.

All the greatness, the idiosyncracies, the horror, the elections and race problems, mass living and war, assassinations and space triumphs of an unusual decade are pieced together by Braverman with irony, compassion, and brilliant cinematic rhetoric.

The film was originally made for CBS's *60 Minutes*, but the top decision-makers decided not to show it, ostensibly claiming that it left out the pill, the Pope, and nudity. Segments of the film, with deletions of certain incidents which were historically embarrassing to Nixon, were later shown on NBC and ABC.

It is a film which everyone should meditate on to see the greatness and grubbiness of man. It is a powerful lesson in history and a painful one in humanity. The emotional reaction to the selection of scenes and the juxtaposition of images will be varied, because Braverman has arranged his own "truths," but no one will be able to deny the explosiveness of *The Sixties*. Seeing man "at work" in this film is a lesson in salvation history, however indirectly it may come across, and in the urgency for more Christian salt and light and mountain-top cities.

Braverman's three-minute panoramic masterpiece, *American Time Capsule*, which captures 200 years of American history in 1,300 visuals (paintings, newspaper headlines, photos, political cartoons, etc.) should also be viewed with *The Sixties*. Cut to the drum solo of Sandy Nelson in the background, the film pulsates and surges with potent images, most of them violent, and the bombardment makes one realize how much of America's history has been concerned with war, making it an apt context for understanding *The Sixties*.

15 minutes

Pyramid Films $18.00

IX. *THE ANTKEEPER*

This is an overpowering allegory of the incarnation done by Rolf Forsberg. To the sensitive man of faith, this film is an overwhelming experience and stunningly dramatizes the inexpressible covenant love of God for man and its peak epiphany in Jesus Christ.

The film opens up on a magnificent garden full of lush vegetation, which is owned by an antkeeper, who is portrayed by a dignified Mexican padrone dressed all in white. His handsome son is by his side. The antkeeper has created some ants with wings and has sent them into his garden to drink the nectar from all the flowers, except for one certain bloom. The ants, however, succumb to the solicitations of an evil person, half man and half woman, who is jealous of the antkeeper, and they drink from the forbidden flower which withers and dies at their touch. In punishment, the antkeeper pulls out their wings and sends them outside the garden to crawl on the ground and to work and toil. They increase and multiply and eventually they begin to fight one another. In brilliant microscopic camera work Forsberg shows a colony of red ants fighting to the death with a colony of black ants, a scene so brutal and devastating that one hesitates to make the allegorical application to man.

The behavior of the ants hurts the antkeeper deeply. Seeing this, his son volunteers to become one of them so as to teach them the ways of love. He is transformed into an ant himself. He lives and grows among the other ants, but eventually they attack and kill him. A queen ant tends his dead body. She becomes pregnant and produces eggs which burst open and reveal a whole new species of ants that now have wings.

The outlines of the allegory are pretty well known to the average Christian, but the metaphor Forsberg has chosen shocks one into an awareness of the proportions of the incarnation event. St. John's verbal jolt, "The Word was made flesh," suddenly becomes astonishingly meaningful when the viewer sees, through means of trick photography, the handsome son transformed into a creeping (and creepy) ant!

The son comes walking through the garden like a giant, the camera catching one immense foot. But then as he continues to walk down the mountain toward the ant colony, he becomes smaller and smaller, and his clothes become more tattered. He finally crawls on a rock, assumes a fetal position, and his transformation takes place. During this entire sequence, the viewer is reminded of numerous Scripture passages relating to the Messiah, especially the one from the Psalms, "Like a giant he ran the course," and St. Paul's famous, "He emptied himself, taking the form of a slave."

For anyone on a spiritual retreat, this film is an absolute must. The cinematography is breathtaking and matches the exquisite sensitivity with which Forsberg allegorically treats the story line. Here is a film which captures the spirit and the reality of the shocking good news of the Christ event.

30 minutes

Cine-Cath $15.00

X. *RIGHT HERE, RIGHT NOW*

From the Revelation Series of the Franciscan Communications Center's TeleKETICS Division, this film shows how a simple, open man, a janitor in an old apartment house, brings new life to the tenants by his respect for them, his service, his self-effacing expressions of love. He becomes in death a sign of revelation and a bond of love to those whose lives he touched. The joyless lives of the prostitute, the homosexual, and the others are given new meaning by the life and death of the janitor, who becomes a symbol of Christ "right here, right now."

The film is most inspiring and puts demands on the Christian viewer to stand before the world, as the *Constitution on the*

Church has declared, as a "witness to the resurrection and life of the Lord Jesus and a sign that God lives." The film also proclaims that the value of one's commitment to Christ and to the world is not measured by one's position in the world but by one's willingness to be present to others, to be of service to them.

15 minutes

| Franciscan Communications Center | $14.00 |
| Public Relations Office, St. Louis | $ 7.00 |

XI. *LEO BEUERMAN*

This film brings home powerfully the dignity and worth inherent in every individual and man's potential to transcend suffering and handicap. Leo is a man who from childhood has been hopelessly malformed and crippled. The ordinary experiences of growing up have been denied him. And yet Leo has grown up with a courage and love and inspirational philosophy of life that healthier men rarely attain.

The viewer relates to Leo in a deeply personal way. This film, far from arousing mere pity for Leo, raises some of the most profound questions about unmerited suffering that have plagued mankind since the Book of Job. Why does the innocent man suffer is such a comprehensive question that it includes all of salvation history from Abel, to the passion and death of Jesus, to some thorny moral problems today, especially abortion and mercy killing. Must suffering be avoided at all costs? Before one answers that question too readily, he should reflect on something that is often ignored or not recognized, namely that much of the creative work of man, as many artistic geniuses have testified, is built upon suffering. Leo's life is creative and far transcends the banal mediocrity that some societies ignorantly equate with happiness.

13 minutes

Centron Educational Films

XII. *WHY MAN CREATES*

This Oscar-winning film, to name just one of the many prizes it has won, was made by Saul Bass and is a rich and subtle series of explorations, episodes and comments on creativity. It is a composite of eight vignettes which attempt to answer the question of why man creates. The eight sections are entitled: the Edifice, Fooling Around, the Process, the Judgment, a Parable, a Digression, the Search, and the Mark. Each section is quite unique and excites one to reflection on the history of creativity, the qualities needed in a creative person, long-term commitment to a creative idea, and the non-conformity of the creative individual, among many other ideas.

Saul Bass has written in answer to the question of what he was trying to say in this film: "I was trying to demonstrate in both the content and form of the film the nature of the creative process. And, in passing, to celebrate the variety, the richness and importance of the creative vision. The intent of the film is to give those who look at it, and who are probably not working (as a life-commitment) in creative areas, a sense of what it *feels* like to work creatively . . . the agony, the frustration, the discipline, the pleasure, the messiness, the orderliness, the failure (and in the case of the scientist) the aberrant nature of time when you are engaged in the process" (*Film: The Creative Eye*, by David Sohn, p. 49).

Bass also makes another comment about the film which might prove fruitful in discussion (p. 58), ". . . two basic ideas . . . form the conclusion of the film . . . the origins of the creative act. We say that the creative act has to be understood as having its sources in two urges which exist simultaneously or individually. Man creates to leave his mark on his time, as a denial of mortality, to say 'Look at me . . . I was here . . .' He also creates out of a need to identify himself, to himself . . . to say, as we say at the end of the film, 'I am unique . . . I am here . . . I am.' "

The film is superb, and each section will delight and challenge.

25 minutes

Pyramid Films $15.00

XIII. *THE GAME*

This film probes the nature of premarital sexual behavior and the psychology of youth with their inner emotional conflicts and uncertain attitudes toward sex and the effect of peer group pressure on thinking and behavior. Peter is a high school student who is challenged by some of his friends about whether he can "make" it with a girl or not, especially with Nicky, an attractive co-ed. He begins to play the game of girl-baiting. A beach party later provides Peter with the opportunity to prove his masculinity. Both he and Nicky, bored with the party, get into his father's car and drive off to a secluded spot where they have intercourse.

The remainder of the film portrays Peter's uncertain awareness of what he has done and his growing consciousness of guilt. There is a loud, energetic basketball game, a boring afternoon flipping through magazines, an unwillingness to go to school in the mornings, all calculated to show Peter's gnawing sense of futility and emptiness. Then there is the scene of the final meeting with Nicky, whom Peter has been avoiding. The camera shows them talking together and Nicky's only comment is, "That's what they said you'd say," as she walks away. Peter later is seen walking the streets attracted by a worker pounding with a pneumatic drill. The final scene shows him at the phone calling up Nicky.

The film is especially direct and strong in its treatment of the conditions and mentality that lead to irresponsible sexual relations. It does not hesitate to show Peter seeking intercourse as an end in itself, as a test to his masculinity, and as an answer to his curiosity. But at the same time the film, through action and through unusual camera technique, shows Peter undergoing the beginnings of adult awareness. The final scene of the telephone call to Nicky suggests Peter's willingness to seek a deeper relationship with Nicky, one arising from his own desire to attain a more psychologically satisfying union. A screening of this film should lead into an honest, open exchange of feelings about sex, its uses and abuses, in each one's life.

27 minutes

Contemporary Films	$ 8.00
Mass Media Ministries	$10.00
ROA Films	$10.00
Univ. of Arizona	$ 3.00
Univ. of Michigan	$ 5.50
Univ. of Minnesota	$ 4.60
Univ. of Missouri	$ 4.50
Univ. of So. California	$ 7.50

XIV. *PENANCE*

Another in the Sacrament Series of the Franciscan Communications Center's TeleKETICS Division, this film portrays a man struggling with his own responsibility and guilt in regard to a traffic accident in which a young girl is badly hurt. At first he tries to rationalize his innocence, but then he comes to an awareness of his guilt, expresses his sorrow to the young girl over his carelessness, and asks her for forgiveness.

A human situation displays all the elements of penance in a way that is both touching and emblematic of divine forgiveness. The film vividly dramatizes the Gospel experience of meeting the forgiving God in a human context. A child's spontaneous love becomes the human symbol of that divine generosity underlying this sacrament of peace. The film's ending brings one to tears and to a realization of the Lord's words of joy over the return of the sinner.

10 minutes

Franciscan Communications Center	$10.00
Public Relations Office, St. Louis	$ 5.00

XV. *THE DANCING PROPHET*

Doug Crutchfield is a black American dancer, living in Copenhagen, Denmark. He is also a prophet who communicates his vision of dance as an expression of faith by dancing the miracles of

Jesus. He expresses his faith by sharing his vision of dance with the crippled and the elderly. Doug's belief is an active, personal Christian love, which contrasts sharply with his father's open and vehement profession of belief in Jesus as Savior. The conflict is never resolved, but Doug's father responds to the work of his prophet-dancing son: "I see God in his hands."

The film is inspiring and shows the unusual quality of service in one man's life, the sharing of his unique talent to bring joy and even release to lives bent by pain. The beautiful dance sequence in a church sanctuary in which Doug, portraying Christ, heals a woman crippled in body and soul who afterward begins to dance with joy, dramatizes the extent of his character and the spiritual dimensions of his life work.

15 minutes

Franciscan Communications Center	$14.00
Public Relations Office, St. Louis	$ 7.00

XVI. *EUCHARIST*

True to their dedicated belief that faith is the search for Christ in all the corners of human experience, the Franciscan Communications Center has produced a magnificent, free-flowing film on the Eucharist that celebrates Christ's life, death and resurrection and explores the dimensions of the Eucharist in everyday human encounters through a juxtaposition of many images. It is impossible to talk about the film, because it is an experience in sight and sound that invites each viewer to re-create the meaning of the eucharistic mystery in his own life. The visual impact is overwhelming and touches, elliptically and incompletely, the profound mysteries of life, stimulating the viewer both to see the recapitulation of all these mysteries in the Eucharist and to bring newness out of all that is.

For those on a retreat, this is a must film, because it sums up visually the meaning of all encounters, both human and divine, giving their source, their meaning, their fulfillment.

9 minutes

Franciscan Communications Center	$10.00
Public Relations Office, St. Louis	$ 5.00

XVII. *THE UNANSWERED QUESTION*

This cinema-verité film is an eye-opener and shows quite ironically the confusion and hesitation many people have about some of the values they profess so unthinkingly. In interview-style, people on the streets were asked their unrehearsed and candid answers to the question: "What is brotherhood?" The results were tragi-comical, for the film-makers uncovered such vagueness and uncertainty and even unwillingness to answer the question that one begins to wonder whether a person's other values are equally as muddled.

The film can spark a heated discussion on values. Some individuals have what Carl Rogers, the psychologist, calls introjected values, values held as fixed concepts, rarely examined or tested, conceptions of others held as their own without experienced scrutiny and consequent internalization. Most values, furthermore, are uncommunicated, because communicated values place demands on the communicator. People are loath to talk sensibly about their values, either because of uncertainty or lack of courage. And so, many values remain inoperative, like the promise of the son in the Gospels who said he would go out to work for his father but never did.

5 minutes

CCM Films $8.50

XVIII. *AWARENESS*

This film by Rolf Forsberg, film creator of the now famous *Parable*, is a cinematic exposition, done in brilliant visual terms, of the ideal in Buddhism that through sensitivity and awareness of the transcendent and redemptive salvation is already present in all of earthly creation. The film allows the viewer to accompany Prince Siddhartha in a modern day limousine driven by a talkative chauffeur who takes the prince outside his sheltered pleasure garden and shows him where and how ordinary men live. The disease, old age, and death he encounters lead him to abandon his royal heritage and to seek a way to cope with human suffering. After a prolonged period of brooding over the misery he has witnessed, Prince Siddhartha becomes "the rarest of human beings, an enlightened man, a Buddha," who achieves "awareness of the life around us—and the life within us," as Forsberg himself narrates throughout the film.

What the Buddha learns is that "life means change," and one must accept it as "a process not a possession," so that by clinging to permanence one ceases to "clutch at illusion." Out of this awareness, there arises a complete knowledge of self, a complete harmony with creation, and a "compassion for all living things," which makes a person see that "life is one" and that "everything is of infinite value." In the process of expounding these truths, Forsberg charms one optically with sumptuous color cinematography of natural beauty which recalls his other brilliant production, *The Antkeeper*, an allegory of the incarnation.

The high point of the film is an enactment of the Japanese Tea Ceremony, or Cha-na-yuh, which to Forsberg is deeply emblematic of the Buddhistic awareness of oneness. The simple ritual basically consists of the host and the guest sitting together in self-imposed silence and sharing themselves in meditation on the infinity within themselves. The gestures of the host in making the tea are highly stylized and find their counterpart in natural phenomena which Forsberg's camera discloses.

The film is not really a treatise on Buddhism. It is more a contemplation of the sacred in empirical reality, in whatever form it assumes. The film is filled with noble truths that are a challenge to man to become more fully human, to see the possibilities within every creature, to live in harmony with the world and with oneself, to realize as one of the Four Noble Truths of Buddhism that one must rise above his cravings and his ignorance to reach that serenity which is one of the pervasive moods of the film. For the Christian there is the realization that the Spirit of the Lord fills the whole world, fills it with the beauty of the Lord Jesus who, as St. Paul says in Colossians, "holds all things in unity." In conjunction with this film, one should also view *Mood of Zen*, narrated by Alan Watts.

30 minutes

Cine-Cath $15.00

XIX. *THE CUBE*

This complex, thought-provoking film, deserving of a second and third showing to allow its multiple meanings to be realized, shows a man—any man, every man—trapped inside the translucent, plastic walls of a cube. The play's intensity builds on a series of surrealistic encounters with diverse visitors coming in and going out of doors through which the man cannot follow, engaging him in nonsense conversations which so confuse him that he fears he is losing touch with reality. Perplexed, bombarded by ideas and changing realities, the man feels lost. But, surprisingly, he takes hold of himself and, with newly gathered confidence, seems to march out of the cube. Finally he is free—or is he?

This film will puzzle one at first, but an in-depth discussion usually brings out the basic meanings which touch upon some profound life-realities: the presence of mind-sets in people, inflexible frames-of-reference which close off the possibility of change and growth; the contrast between truth and illusion, often blurred by prejudices, preconceived notions, comforting lies, and failed communication on every level; the world of one's values, uncommunicated, ambiguous, inoperative; the area of failed potentialities, both intrapersonal and interpersonal, which produce guilt; and the whole notion of freedom, whether one has the right to sovereignty, unfettered liberty, or autonomy, freedom curtailed out of social awareness and respect. The ending of the film is quite surprising and produces even more questions.

56 minutes

NBC Educational Enterprises $19.00

XX. *BAPTISM*

This film, based on a true incident, is subtitled the "Sacrament of Belonging" and is part of the Sacrament Series of the Franciscan Communications Center's TeleKETICS Division. It features a young boy by the name of Alfredo, badly scarred in the face by fire and homeless, who yearns for the warmth and love he sees among the children of the "hacienda." He wanders in and almost hesitatingly asks to join them, fearing that they might reject him because of his disfigured face. His request is answered with the simple declaration: "You are my brother." At this, joy suffuses Alfredo's face; and the rest of the children, with laughter on their faces, join in welcoming a new member of the family.

Again, as with others in the Sacrament Series, this film presents the mystery of divine friendship in a human setting. It recalls Christ's potent words: "I call you friends."

10 minutes

Franciscan Communications Center $10.00
Public Relations Office, St. Louis $ 5.00

XXI. *THE STRINGBEAN*

This film by Edmond Sechan, considered France's greatest poet of the screen, tells the tender story of an old Parisian seamstress who lives alone in a dark, drab, walk-up apartment. One day she retrieves a discarded flowerpot from the garbage heap, takes it to her room and plants a single bean in the pot's soil. Under her loving care the bean begins to sprout, and the old lady tries to expose the young leaves to every patch of sun that she can find in her small room. When the plant sprouts so many leaves that it needs more sun than the apartment can afford, the old lady walks the numerous stairs up and down to take the plant outside and sit with it in the park for several days. When she realizes that the plant is getting too large for the pot, she furtively transplants it among the beautiful flowers in a well-tended park. Eventually, the gardeners discover the bean plant, rip it out, and discard it among the weeds. The old woman, who has been sitting nearby each day watching the plant thrive in the sunlight and excellent soil, rushes over and picks a few stringbeans from the discarded stalk. She then goes home and plants three new pod seeds in the flowerpot.

The implications of the film are numerous, arising both from the story line and the cinematic technique. With regard to technique, when the woman is in her drab room the footage is in black and white; when she is outside in the sunlight, the film is in color, emphasizing life and the conditions for growth in contrast to the constricted, lonely existence of a life without love. The story line, in which the old lady tenderly nourishes a tiny plant, is an eloquent portrayal of the need human beings have to cherish another living creature so that it may blossom to full potential. Her loving care reminds one of Viktor Frankl's beautiful words in his book *Man's Search for Meaning*:

> Love is the only way to grasp another human being in the innermost core of his personality. No one can become fully aware of the very essence of another human being unless he loves him. By the spiritual act of love he is enabled to see the essential traits and features in the beloved person; and even more, he sees that which is potential in him, that which is not yet actualized but yet ought to be actualized. Furthermore, by his love, the loving person enables the beloved person to actualize these potentialities. By making him aware of what he can be and of what he should become, he makes these potentialities come true.

The film has also a great deal to say about old age and loneliness, the sadness in the remembrance of things past and yet the hope that love given brings others near and love received makes one young again. In a certain sad sense, the careless gardeners who unfeelingly uproot the living beanstalk because it does not fit in represent those who would discard anything apparently useless, old, worn-out. They lack the imagination to realize that the necessity to care is a condition for true living in others. Here, one is reminded of the words of Christ in the parable of the Last Judgment, where he identifies himself with the least likely of the world (Matthew 25:31-46). One also recalls the parable of the Good Samaritan which seemingly Christ gave to show that, whereas the poor beaten man on the road was in no way close to the Samaritan, because the Samaritan made the necessary move ("he was moved with compassion"), he became near to him and thus helped him to live truly.

17 minutes

Contemporary Films

XXII. *JUST LIKE YOU*

With the haunting voice of Eugene Osborne Smith narrating against a montage of photographic portraits and scenes of daily life from around the world, this powerful film stresses that all people—rich, poor, black, red, brown, white, yellow—are all "just like you" in their desire for love and respect, for rewarding and meaningful lives, for a chance to express in freedom and dignity their shared hopes and dreams. The faces shown are magnificent portraits of various races, all etched nobly in suffering and hard work, and they speak eloquently of man's feelings, his concerns, his quest for understanding and help, love of life, all challenging the viewer to see and understand that "I am . . . just like you!"

The film makes the definite point that only through awareness and sensitivity to others can one develop the ability to understand and appreciate life and the world around him. The film inspires reflection on the need for love, respect and friendship and, especially, an appreciation and deep admiration for different cultures and different social frames of reference. It also profoundly challenges one to a common understanding of a common sacred heritage: humanness. The film vividly recalls the words of the Lord: "You are all brothers."

6 minutes

Stephen Bosustow Productions

XXIII. *SCRAP OF PAPER AND A PIECE OF STRING*

This film tells of the friendship between a scrap of paper and a piece of string, the original Dixieland score in the background highlighting their antics in assuming many shapes and sizes. The scrap of paper becomes inordinately proud of its possibilities, much to the dismay of the piece of string, whose self-image is badly hit. One day the scrap of paper, in assuming the shape of a ship, is blown too far out onto a small body of water and is in danger of being waterlogged and drowned. The string comes to the rescue by attaching itself around a nearby tree and throwing itself out into the water to tow in the embarrassed and much chastened scrap of paper.

This beautifully designed film speaks to one about interpersonal involvement, openness to relatedness with others, and authentic intimacy as necessary conditions for self-actualization and preservation from drowning in the waters of narcissism. It also says a great deal about those who are skilled at impersonal, instrumental role-playing and introverted self-delineation, but who never confirm their fellowman in his very being. What is significant in the short film is that the scrap of paper's death of its illusion led to a rebirth of strength, that its near loss of identity was saved by capitulating to the out-reach of the other. The scrap of paper also realized the hidden, hitherto unrecognized powers in the piece of string, and the piece of string received confirmation of its own true self-concept that it also was a loving and capable being.

The film illustrates the often unrealized truth that there is greatness in every human being, if only others had the imaginative eyes to see it. One is reminded here of the story of Zaccheus the Publican sitting up in the tree to get a glimpse of the Lord. It seems that no one thought too highly of him and so he expected nothing of anyone; but when the Lord came by, recognized him, and said, "Zaccheus, hurry down; I'm staying at your house today," Zaccheus became a new man. Someone—and someone significant at that—had noticed.

5 minutes   Contemporary Films McGraw-Hill

XXIV. *EVASION*

This inspiring film is reminiscent of *The Red Balloon* in beauty of photography and delicacy of statement. It tells the story of a young boy who discovers a marionette, actually a man dehumanized by the impersonal forces of urban life. He leads it out of the shop into the open countryside and puts the marionette in contact with living creatures. This discovery of nature restores the marionette and he becomes a man again and begins to dance for joy.

The themes of the film are numerous and suggest thoughts and feelings on love, friendship, contemplation, freedom, the importance of beauty, the possible destructive effects of urbanized living. The film can also be discussed from the aspects of baptism and resurrection.

17 minutes

Kohpri Films, Paris (Public Library)

XXV. *MOOD OF ZEN*

Beautiful photography of the man-made and the natural in Japan supports the thesis of Alan Watts, the film's narrator, that Zen Buddhism is a system that gives man modes of consciousness suited for his role in the community of nature. What is needed is for man to realize that he must not impose himself on the land but must build and act in harmony with the forces and energy of the world.

Western man, as Alan Watts has said in another place, has a tendency to remain in subjective isolation because he separates himself from the idea of himself, a mind-body dualism that ends up by identifying one's actual self with the idea of one's self. Hence the subjective feeling of a "self" which "has" a mind. Zen Buddhism, with its emphasis on the concrete, points out that when one is no longer identified with the idea of oneself, "the entire relationship between subject and object, knower and known, undergoes sudden and revolutionary change. It becomes a real relationship, a mutuality in which the subject creates the object just as much as the object creates the subject. The knower no longer feels himself to be independent of the known, the experiencer no longer feels himself to stand apart from the experience. Consequently, the whole notion of getting something 'out' of life, of seeking something 'from' experience, becomes absurd. To put it in another way, it becomes vividly clear that in concrete fact I have no other self than the totality of things of which I am aware" (*The Way of Zen*).

Although it is not necessary to understand the above to appreciate the film, it does help to clarify Alan Watts' comments in the film. It is an entirely different frame of reference, a completely different mode of structuring the world, which Alan Watts speaks about in this film, a world view that is full of beauty and serenity and harmony and bears out the statements of Thomas Merton about the necessity for Western man to appreciate Eastern thought. He writes, "If the West continues to underestimate and to neglect the spiritual heritage of the East, it may hasten the tragedy that threatens man and his civilization" (*Mystics and Zen Masters*).

This film has the effect of inspiring the viewer to take a fresh look at nature, to become aware of its grace and beauty and patterned movements. Only man, as Alan Watts says in the film, is capable of an ungraceful motion. The latter part of the film emphasizes the flowing quality of water, its rich symbolic quality in Zen mysticism, and recalls to mind a warning to man not to push the river, since it flows by itself.

13 minutes

Hartley Productions

INDEX FOR ALL THREE VOLUMES

THEME	TALK	EXERCISE	LITURGY	HOMILY	FILM
Lifestyle		III-38, 52			
Loneliness					III-183, 195
Love	II-72, 154	II-222, III-41, 42		II-222, 226	III-187, 195, 198
Marriage	II-154, 240, 244ff	II-260		III-170	
Mary	I-63				
Mercy			I-99, II-110		
Nature					III-198
Neighbor	I-78ff, II-77, 99	II-106	I-100		
Openness					III-185
Passion to Resurrection	II-89				
Peace	II-32ff	II-190			
Penance			I-85, II-208 III-116	II-209 III-149	III-191
Person		I-142, 184	III-40		
Poverty					III-182
Prayer	I-65, 112	I-175	I-34	I-122, III-151	
Prejudice		II-221		III-153	II-212, III-24
Presence of God	II-8		III-139		
Racism				III-152	
Relationship	II-111	II-253, III-29-30, 31, 50			III-181
Religious Traditions	I-163ff				
Responsibility					III-83, 180, 195
Resurrection	II-94, 135				III-188
Rosary		I-89			
Sacraments	I-61, II-143				III-191, 192, 195
Saint Francis				II-32	
Salvation	I-29ff, II-134				III-193
Scripture	II-57				
New Testament	II-60, 66, 74, 78, 83, 88, 96, 102, 132				
Old Testament	II-52ff, 127ff				
Search for God	II-10, III-4ff				III-32
Self-Image & Confidence	II-77, 99				
Service	I-78ff	II-106	I-100	II-205	III-182
Sexuality	I-115, II-156		I-96	I-122	III-190
Spiritual Life	II-10, 13, 17				
Suffering					III-182
Time		III-45	III-141		
Unity			III-135		
Values	II-23, 183	II-171, 257 III-100ff			III-192
—Interpersonal Process		II-176			
—Personal		II-235			
—Religious		II-178, 188			
—Clarification	I-136	I-137ff			

THEME	TALK	EXERCISE	LITURGY	HOMILY	FILM
Violence					III-180, 183
Vows	I-70ff		I-100	I-123, 124	
War		II-190			III-180
Way of Cross				III-121	
Witness	II-94				
Women	I-104ff			I-121	
Wonder					III-198

GENERAL BOOKBINDING CO.

78   193NY2   4   340   A   2V   6321

QUALITY CONTROL MARK